When a Ghost Talks, Listen

A CHOCTAW
TRAIL OF TEARS STORY

THE HOW I BECAME A GHOST SERIES
BOOK 2

Tim Tingle

THE ROADRUNNER PRESS
OKLAHOMA CITY

Published by The RoadRunner Press
Oklahoma City, Oklahoma
www.TheRoadRunnerPress.com

Map by Steven Walker / Cover design by Jeanne Devlin

This is a work of fiction. While the literary perceptions and insights are based on experience, all names, characters, places, and incidents are either products of the author's imagination or are used fictitiously. No reference to any real person is intended or should be inferred.

First Edition: August 2018
Printed in the USA

ISBN 978-1-937054-51-9 (HC) | ISBN 978-1-937054-69-4 (TP)

Library of Congress Control Number: 2017952749

Publisher's Cataloging-In-Publication Data
(Prepared by The Donohue Group, Inc.)

Names: Tingle, Tim. | Walker, Steven (Illustrator), illustrator.
Title: When a ghost talks, listen : a Choctaw Trail of Tears story / Tim Tingle ; map by Steven Walker.
Description: Oklahoma City : The RoadRunner Press, [2018] | Series: The how I became a ghost series ; book 2 | Interest age level: 9 and up. | Includes bibliographical references. | Summary: "Ten-year-old Isaac, now a ghost, continues with his people as they walk the Choctaw Trail of Tears headed to Indian Territory in what will one day become Oklahoma. There have been surprises aplenty on their trek, but now Isaac and his three Choctaw comrades learn they can time travel--making for an unexpected adventure. The foursome heads back in time to Washington, D.C., to bear witness for Choctaw Chief Pushmataha who has come to the nation's capital at the invitation of Andrew Jackson."--Provided by publisher.
Identifiers: ISBN 978-1-937054-51-9 | ISBN 978-1-937054-65-6 (ebook)
Subjects: LCSH: Choctaw Indians--Relocation--Juvenile fiction. | Indian Removal, 1813-1903--Juvenile fiction. | Ghosts--Juvenile fiction. | Time travel--Juvenile fiction. | Choctaw Nation of Oklahoma--Juvenile fiction. | CYAC: Choctaw Indians--Fiction. | Ghosts--Fiction. | Time travel--Fiction. | LCGFT: Historical fiction.
Classification: LCC PZ7.T489 Wh 2017 (print) | LCC PZ7.T489 (ebook) | DDC [Fic]--dc23

Dedicated to
the hard-working students
of Jones Academy

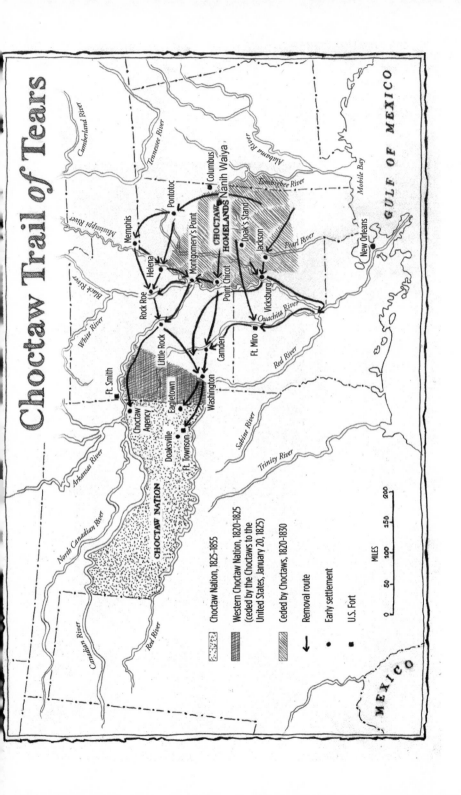

Choctaw Trail of Tears

GULF OF MEXICO

MEXICO

Cumberland River
Tennessee River
Mississippi River
Alabama River
Black River
White River
Ouachita River
Red River
Arkansas River
North Canadian River
Canadian River
Red River
Sabine River
Trinity River
Pearl River
Tombigbee River

Columbus
Pontotoc
Memphis
Helena
Rock Roe
Montgomery's Point
Point Chicot
Nanih Waiya
Doak's Stand
Jackson
Vicksburg
Ft. Miro
Camden
Little Rock
Ft. Smith
Choctaw Agency
Eagletown
Doaksville
Ft. Towson
Washington
New Orleans

Mobile Bay

CHOCTAW HOMELANDS

CHOCTAW NATION

Choctaw Nation, 1825–1855

Western Choctaw Nation, 1820–1825
(ceded by the Choctaws to the
United States, January 20, 1825)

Ceded by Choctaws, 1820–1830

→ Removal route

• Early settlement

■ U.S. Fort

MILES

0   50   100   150   200

Chapter 1

Choctaw Ghosts are Everywhere
Leaving Choctaw Nation, 1830

SINCE YOU'RE READING my second book, you already know who I am. You know my name is Isaac, that I'm ten years old, soon to be eleven, and you know I am a ghost. I am not dead, not in the usual way. I am not buried and gone, but I am a ghost.

I have learned to travel by closing my eyes and thinking where I want to be. That's how ghosts do it. I can disappear so no one can see me or I can gradually float into sight, as you will recall. But I didn't tell you everything about being a ghost. I didn't want to terrify you. But you're older now—you can handle it.

Do not be afraid of what I am about to say.

Whenever you read a book about Choctaw ghosts, Choctaw ghosts are always with you, surrounding you and sometimes even reading over your shoulder. Yes, even now, a Choctaw ghost is peering over your shoulder. Whatever you do, **DO NOT LOOK OVER YOUR RIGHT SHOULDER.**

Don't be afraid. The ghosts are there to protect you. Just say halito ("hello" in Choctaw) and keep reading. If a ghost taps you on the shoulder, simply smile and wave backwards.

Hoke, I still have friends who are ghosts and friends who are people. Like Joseph. He's a real teenager, but sometimes he can be a panther, and sometimes he can be a sixteen-year-old. If you think that sounds crazy, trust me—it's even crazier than you think. But he's still my best friend.

Nita is another friend of mine. She rolled out of her blanket one night and froze in the snow, so she's a ghost like me, even though she's only five years old. Her mother and father, Ruth and Gabe, are my parents' best friends.

Nita's older sister, Naomi, is a teenager like Joseph, but she's not a panther and she's not a ghost. She feels the cold and walks the trail with a thousand other Choctaws.

And before I forget, my dog Jumper still walks the trail, though having a dog has become a little complicated since I became a ghost, as Jumper is quick to remind me.

"We need to talk," Jumper said one morning.

We were following a winding road through the forest, an hour after breakfast.

"What's up?"

"I liked you better when you were a boy," Jumper said.

"Why?" I asked him. "Now that I'm invisible, I can sneak up on the soldiers. I can watch what they do, listen to what they say, and they never even know I'm around."

"Yeah," Jumper said. "That's hoke." (Jumper speaks English and Choctaw.)

"Then what's the problem?"

"Well," said Jumper, "now that you're a ghost you never eat anymore. I don't want to complain, but when you ate breakfast along with everybody else, you always made sure I had plenty to eat."

Jumper was right. Now that I wasn't eating anymore, I never stayed around to watch everybody else eat at mealtime. My mother and dad, my big brother Luke, and little Nita's family always ate together around the same campfire.

"I'm sorry, Jumper," I said. "You know ghosts don't eat, and I just forget sometimes."

"I forgive you," Jumper said, "but I am still hungry."

"Why don't you ask Luke to give you something to eat?"

Jumper didn't say a word. He just tilted his head and rolled his eyes back. That's dog talk for *I think you know the answer to that one.*

"Oh, right," I said. Luke was a great big brother, but he couldn't understand dog talk. "I'll mention it to Luke and remind him to feed you."

"Yakoke," Jumper said. ("Thank you" in Choctaw.)

"I'll make sure you get something special for supper," I said. "Fried squirrel, how would you like that?"

"Sounds hoke to me," Jumper said, with a wag of his tail.

"Now, you want to help me find Joseph?" I asked. "I haven't seen him since yesterday morning. When he's gone that long, he's usually Panther Joseph, climbing trees and exploring."

Jumper wagged his tail hoke, and we turned to the woods. Before I took another step, a white cloud appeared in front of me and General Pushmataha stepped from it.

"Isaac," Pushmataha said, "you are a smart young man and a quick learner. I have chosen a task for you and your friends."

I knew better than to ask what task. Choctaw elders will tell you what they want you to know when they are ready and not before. General Pushmataha smiled at my patience.

"You still have much to learn about being a ghost," he said. "I would like to take you on a long trip into the past. And even though they are among the living, I would like Naomi and Joseph to join us later. And someone else with strange powers will help us as well."

He stared at me once more, knowing the question was burning in my chest.

"Nita?" I finally asked.

"No," he said. "Nita needs to stay with her family. They need her more than ever now that she's a ghost."

I clinched my lips together tight. I rocked back and forth. Hoke, I could already see this was going to be a game General Pushmataha played. He knows the answer and I have to shut up and wait. Maybe he was trying to teach me something about listening rather than talking all the time. I put one hand under my chin and the other on top of my head and pushed. Hard. It was impossible to talk. Go ahead; try it if you don't believe me.

General Pushmataha laughed so hard he almost fell over backwards. He even put his hands on his own chin and head, making fun of me! Generals aren't supposed to make fun of little kid ghosts, are they?

"Isaac," he said, "I knew I liked you the first time I saw you."

"When was that?"

"When you stuffed your shirt with snow and icicles, pretending to be a Snow Monster to scare your dog."

"You saw that? You were there?"

"Of course, Isaac," Pushmataha said. "A good Choctaw leader has to know how to laugh, and you make it easy."

"Yakoke," I said. "I guess."

"Do you remember Stella?" he asked. "The Choctaw councilwoman?"

I nodded.

"Achukma ('good' in Choctaw)," he said. "Remember the day the Nahullos were so mean to everyone? Leader blasted a tree branch with his shotgun, and it fell on Stella. He would not allow anyone to help her."

I saw what happened that day as if it were in front of my eyes. Joseph and I were hiding deep in the woods. Joseph was so mad he wanted to turn into a panther and knock Leader from his horse.

11

"Isaac, you never want to make an elder Choctaw woman your enemy. Never. Do you understand me?"

"Yes," I whispered.

"Achukma," he continued. "Especially Stella. Do you remember the rattlesnake that protected Nita, after she died? Leader wanted to harm her body in front of her grieving parents. Remember?"

"The rattlesnake? That was Stella?" I asked.

"That's right," General Pushmataha said. "That was Stella."

Pushmataha shook his head and laughed. He was enjoying this game way too much.

"Don't you think Stella the Rattlesnake is a good person to have around?"

"Ummmm," I said, determined to use as few words as possible.

"Isaac," he said, with a serious look of wrinkled brows and tight lips. "Even a sound is talking. When that dog of yours growls and barks, that is his way of talking."

"No!" I shouted. "General Pushmataha, Jumper does talk. He can talk in Choctaw and English and dog talk, too. He makes more sense that most of the people I know. Jumper does not growl and bark, he says people words."

The general never changed his expression. "I think I just tricked you into talking, Little Isaac."

"That's not funny," I said. "Hoke, that was a little bit funny."

"Achukma," he said. "Now that we have had our laugh, it's time to make our plans."

I folded my arms across my knees and leaned in close to listen.

Chapter 2
Rattlesnake Stella

BEFORE GENERAL PUSHMATAHA could say a word, I heard the rustling of dried leaves. I was too scared to look, but I finally realized that whatever it was, it couldn't hurt me now. I'm a ghost. I glanced to my right and there she sat, curled up with her fangs drooping and her head resting on her rattles. I looked to Pushmataha and pointed to the snake. He read the question in my eyes.

"Yes, Isaac. That is Stella."

As if in response, the rattlesnake wriggled her tail and a soft *whirrrr* filled the silence.

"I have invited Stella to be a guardian while you and I travel," said Pushmataha.

I puffed my chest and smiled a big smile. General Pushmataha, maybe the most famous Choctaw of all time, had chosen me to join him on a dangerous journey. Then—as quick as a firefly—I hung my head in shame. This was no time for me to be proud. Yes, I am a tushka shilombish, a spirit warrior, but I will never be a great one like him, General Pushmataha. "I will do my best," I said.

General Pushmataha touched my shoulder. "You will do fine, Isaac. I have been watching you for longer than you know."

"Will Nita be hoke?" I asked.

"Isaac," he said, "Nita will not be alone. She is such a cute little girl; she'll have a thousand Choctaw ohoyos (ohoyo is "woman" in Choctaw) scrambling to take care of her. But that task will fall on one very special ohoyo, our Choctaw councilwoman."

The snake lifted her head and tail at the same time. She gave a rattle, pointed her pointy-head in my direction, and waved her fangs at me.

Hoke, ghost or not, I was afraid.

"It's only Stella," said Pushmataha, trying not to laugh.

I did my best to smile at her, but I had been trained from childhood to make no sudden movements around a rattlesnake. Even though this was Stella, she was still a snake. "Maybe my brother, Luke, can look out for Nita," I suggested.

This did not please Rattlesnake Stella. Her head froze, and she stared at me with unblinking eyes. The whole world froze, for just a moment, and then Stella drew her head back as if to strike.

Maybe I didn't stay as still as I thought. Maybe I

flinched. Maybe. But that does not excuse what Stella did. She flung her fangs at me, dripping with rattlesnake venom.

"Noooo!" I shouted, expecting the worst pain in the world, the pain of poison fangs sinking into my skin. Of course, I had no skin and could feel no pain. Rattlesnake Stella and General Pushmataha just laughed. At me!

Stella slithered into the general's lap. I tried my best to be mad, watching the most honored of all Choctaw chiefs, now a ghost, and a Choctaw councilwoman, now a rattlesnake, share laughter at my expense. Finally, I did what any good Choctaw would do. I joined them. We all had a good laugh, a good Choctaw laugh.

"I think that settles it," Pushmataha said. "Stella will look out for Nita while we travel. That hoke, Isaac?"

"Achukma, good," I said.

He nodded at Stella, and she slipped down to the ground and wriggled away in the tall grass.

I still don't know where we are going, I thought.

"Glad you asked, Isaac," said Pushmataha. He brushed a mosquito from his nose and glanced to the treetops.

How does he do that? I wondered. I'd given up trying to swat mosquitoes as a ghost a long time ago.

"You ready to go, Isaac?"

Before I could open my mouth to answer, I was floating a hundred feet above the trees. I didn't close my eyes; I didn't even blink. I wanted to see everything. The world and sky and everything turned dark, but not a black lights-out dark.

No, this dark swirled with color. Yellow and red and blinding white, then briefly black as night. I felt neither dizzy nor strange as I sat and watched the kaleidoscope of flashing colors, green and purple and sky blue, too.

"Halito," I whispered. "Hello."

"I'm here," Pushmataha said. "We are hoke, Isaac."

I could no longer feel the wind, but I knew it was blowing. My body tumbled like a leaf in a tornado, upside down and around and around. I put my hand to my mouth to keep from throwing up and sending regurgitated corn like yellow raindrops on the walkers below. *That's dumb*, I thought. *Ghosts don't eat, so ghost can't vomit!*

And then, for the first time in several days, I felt the shiver. I closed my eyes, but when I opened them I saw nothing I hadn't seen before. Yet something was different. I heard a voice, as soft as a songbird in the roar of the storm.

Soon whispering voices came from all directions, surrounding me. The singing settled everything. I smiled to hear the song "Shilombish Holitopama," "Amazing Grace" in Choctaw.

Through the mist, older men and women circled all around me. Their heads were bowed, and their palms were lifted to the high heavens as they sang.

Shilombish Holitopama
Ish minti pullacha
Hattak lbasha iyaha
Ishpi yukpa lashki

How could I feel afraid? The wind blew gently and I stopped rolling.

I opened my eyes and saw the earth below, through fleeting holes in a cloud. We sailed over mountains covered in tall pine trees. Sometimes we flew high above the mountaintops and other times so close to the forests below that I could have leapt onto a tree limb.

We slowed down as a sparkling river came into view, winding like a snake through the forest. Small canoes and fishing boats floated up and down the river.

So this is what it's like to be a hawk, I thought. Soaring up and diving down, from clouds to earth and back again. I wonder what it's like at night?

Suddenly a ball of fire dropped from the sky. I expected the woods to explode in flames and to see foxes and squirrels flee from the fire. But nothing burned. Nothing. Instead, everything turned dark. A yellow moon glowed on deep blue waters, surrounded by twinkling silver stars.

I realized I had just watched a sunset, the fastest sunset ever. Wait till I tell Joseph.

I had never seen a world so beautiful. I was beginning to understand why ghosts are so much happier than people. Even though death surrounds us, so does life, and life is an adventure—one exciting moment after another.

Chapter 3
He Rides a White Horse

THE RIVER SOON widened and flowed into a bay. "We're almost there," Pushmataha said. As if he had made it happen, the glowing ball of fire lifted to the sky, slower this time.

Maybe we'll land soon, I thought.

Less than four seconds later, we stood beneath a fat oak tree. Thick limbs hung almost to the ground. A tall stone fence surrounded us and gravestones were scattered up and down narrow paths.

I heard the sound of drums, many drums. I had heard of armies marching into battle, but never had I seen anything like this. Across the graveyard, soldiers entered through an iron gate. First came the drummers, followed by men in fancy uniforms riding horses. The horses stepped high, almost dancing. Next came the marching soldiers, with their guns held over their shoulders. The soldiers marched to the beat of the drums, lifting their feet high and pounding their boots to the ground.

I looked at General Pushmataha. He held his head high too, just like the officers riding the horses. He slapped his hands against his thighs to the beat of the drummers. *He is one of them*, I thought. *He wants to be with them.*

But I was wrong. He did not want to be with them. A loud cheering sound rose from the crowd outside the gate. A man riding a white horse entered the graveyard, dressed in a blue uniform and holding his hat under his left arm. His head was tilted in pride and his long white hair blew in the breeze.

"General Andrew Jackson," Pushmataha whispered.

A wagon entered the gate behind the new general, pulled by six strong ponies. Pushmataha froze upon seeing the wagon. It carried a long box made of shiny wood.

I have seen so many suffer on the walk. I had watched the creeping sickness and the fires that took so many lives. But what I now saw was different.

General Pushmataha's suffering came from inside him. It was the suffering caused by memories. Slowly he lifted his palms to his cheeks. His eyes shifted back and forth, from General Jackson to the wooden box.

I wanted to know who was in the box, but I was afraid to ask. *Whoever it is, he's very important to Pushmataha*, I thought. For the second time that day, I felt the shiver, and I bowed my head out of respect for what I was about to see. When I opened my eyes we were standing in the middle of twenty ghost soldiers, maybe more. But these soldiers were Choctaws. They wore the same uniforms as the living soldiers, but they were Choctaws.

Suddenly, I realized: These Choctaw soldiers wore the same uniforms as the soldiers making us walk in the freezing snow, away from our homes.

Why? I thought.

General Pushmataha glanced at me. I will explain later, his glance seemed to say.

He waited as the Choctaw soldiers formed a line in front of him. He then walked from one to the other. Each in his turn gave him a strong salute. Soon all turned their eyes to the wagon carrying the box.

I had to know. I closed my eyes and wished myself into the box. When I opened my eyes a few seconds later, I was floating over a body, and I would have given anything not to have entered the box.

"Nooo," I cried, and tears flowed down my cheeks. Ghost tears. Stretched out in the box, in the full uniform of a general in the United States Army, was Pushmataha. His face was swollen and red and his eyes were closed.

Why did we come here? I asked myself. *Why?*

"Because you need to know," Pushmataha said. "I have brought you here to teach you, Isaac."

I left the box and stood by his side.

The Choctaw ghost soldiers, still standing at attention, surrounded us. Pushmataha touched his fingers to my face and wiped my tears away.

"I am so sorry," I said.

"So am I, Isaac, but for a different reason. I trusted the man who rides the white horse, the man with so much pride. He was my friend, or so I thought. He betrayed us, all of us."

The wagon carrying the casket came to a halt by a hole in the ground. Two men stood nearby, gripping shovels and waiting to toss dirt on the casket once the ceremony was over.

Soon the graveyard was crowded with people, hundreds of people, all straining to catch a glimpse of the man riding the white horse.

"That's him!" a young man shouted, lifting his daughter onto his shoulders. "That is General Andrew Jackson! Senator Andrew Jackson!"

Jackson never looked at all the people staring at him. He heard them say his name, but he held his chin high and his nose in the air.

A thin man with thick eyeglasses, carrying a Bible under his arm, walked behind the wagon. When the procession stopped, he walked around and stood by the grave. Four soldiers lifted the coffin from the wagon, set it by the hole, and moved quickly to stand by the gravediggers.

"We are here today to pay honor to a great American soldier—General Pushmataha," said the thin man, holding the Bible high. "He fought the British invaders, serving under General Andrew Jackson in the Battle of New Orleans. He will now forever lie in a place of honor, the Congressional Cemetery of the United States of America."

A soldier stepped forward with a bugle under his arm. General Jackson nodded to the bugler, who lifted his instrument and played a slow song as the soldiers raised the coffin once more, then lowered it into the ground.

General Jackson stepped from his horse and approached the grave. A soldier rushed from the line and handed him a cluster of long-stemmed roses. The general knelt over the coffin, whispered a few words, and dropped the roses on the wooden casket.

I wanted to know what General Jackson said, so I closed my eyes and shivered myself into the recent past. I knelt beside General Jackson and heard him say, "May you rest in peace."

I flashed myself into the present and stood beside our Choctaw general, our chief, and I heard his reply.

"I will never rest in peace," General Pushmataha said. "My people need me, and I will always be there for them. We are Choctaws, we know what you did, and we will never rest in peace."

Chapter 4

Panther in the Past

WE STOOD SILENTLY, watching until the last shovel of dirt was tossed on our general's coffin.

"Yakoke for joining me," Pushmataha said to the ghost soldiers. "Now let us return to the walking and take care of the living ones."

Once more, I rose into the air. I rolled and tumbled like a leaf in a storm, watching the sun explode into daylight and disappear in blinding darkness. With a loud *whoosh*, I felt my ears rip from my head!

Hoke, I thought, *this is new.* Like bees buzzing over a field of flowers, my ears flipped and flashed and spun around my head, tapping me on the nose and slapping my cheeks. "How are you doing that?" I asked. I knew who the culprit was.

"You have to remember, Isaac," Pushmataha said, "I'm an old man. I've been around a while."

"Hoke," I said. "You are my elder and I know this must be fun, but can I please have my ears back?"

Before the words left my lips, I felt my ears digging holes into the side of my head. But I'm a ghost, so I felt no pain.

"Let's see how smart you are, young Isaac," Pushmataha said. "What have you learned about me?"

I thought for a long time before I answered. I stopped swirling in the sky, and the ghost of Pushmataha appeared, seated beside me on a puffy cloud. He had a warm smile and tilted his head, waiting for me to answer. *I could make a joke*, I thought, *but he asked a serious question.*

"I know you are a strong leader," I said.

"Yakoke," he said. "But you already knew that, Isaac. What else have you learned?"

"I learned that you were betrayed by a man you trusted, and that hurts you."

"What else?"

I tried to remember everything Pushmataha had said and done since we began our travels through time. "I learned that you are like my father," I finally replied.

"How?"

"When terrible things happen, when our house burned down and we walked in the freezing snow, my father always tried to make us happy. Somehow he wanted my brother and me to still laugh and joke. That's why he pretended to be a Snow Monster."

"I never did anything like that," Pushmataha said, with a serious look on his face.

"You're doing it right now," I said. "You know what I'm talking about. You and Rattlesnake Stella had fun with me, and you did it again when you ripped my ears off."

"Why would I do that?"

"Because that is what we do, we Choctaws," I said. "We never let the bad take over."

Pushmataha nodded and gave me a warm smile of respect. "Yes, Isaac. Your mother and father are proud of you, as am I. You are growing and learning."

The twinkle returned to his eyes, and I knew something was about to happen. I looked below and saw myself dropping through the clouds. The trees were heavy with icicles and the ground was covered in frozen snow. I saw campfires burning. Choctaws huddled close, their blankets wrapped tight around them.

"It must be morning," I whispered.

A forest of oak trees rushed at me from below. I reached my palms in front of me, grabbed a tree, and wrapped my arms around its thick trunk.

Somehow I stopped. I clung to the tree with my ghost arms. I didn't fall to the ground like before. How did I do that?

"You *thought* yourself hanging onto the tree trunk," Pushmataha said. "That's how a ghost does things, Isaac. You *think* and you *do* at the same time. Or better yet," he added, "try thinking before you act, Isaac."

He laughed that gentle Pushmataha laugh and slowly

disappeared, but the sound of his voice stayed behind, repeating over and over, "Think before you act, Isaac. Think before you act."

As if in reply, the icy leaves above me rattled and fell to the ground. I looked up and saw Joseph, hidden among the branches—Panther Joseph.

"Joseph, come down and let's talk," I said.

No matter how many times I see Joseph turn from a panther to a teenager, I always stand in awe and stare. He landed on the ground on all four paws, then bent his knees and eased into a crouch, close to the ground.

Little by little, patches of human skin appeared all over his body. The strangest thing of all was happening on his face. Long panther whiskers grew shorter, like black pins sticking in Joseph's face. Yet Joseph showed no pain; he merely crouched and waited. His pointed ears lost their point and slid from the top of his head to halfway down his skull, settling there like yours and mine.

Hoke, are you ready for this? The panther rose on his hind legs. His paws became fingers and hands and before I knew it, Joseph stood before me, dressed and ready for action.

"Where have you been?" he asked. "I've been looking all over for you."

"I've been with General Pushmataha," I said. "I guess it's hoke to tell you this."

Joseph gave me a look that said *I'm still your best friend, right? We tell each other everything.*

"We went back in time. I know this sounds hashimbo

("crazy" in Choctaw), and it was. We went to Washington, the capitol for Nahullos, the city where Pushmataha is buried. Joseph, I went to his funeral."

"What was it like, traveling in time?"

"Faster than the fastest deer. So fast the sun rose and set and the days flew by, and I was blinded by it all. When everything finally slowed down, we floated into a graveyard. I saw Pushmataha's body being buried, Joseph. He stood by me and watched and was so sad."

"I would be sad, too," Joseph said. "You saw his body?"

"Yes, I floated inside the coffin and saw him. But that is not the worst thing I saw," I said. I didn't even want to tell him about the man who rode the white horse. I had been so mad when I saw Pushmataha staring at that man, a man he once trusted like I trust Joseph.

"What is it, Isaac?"

"I think I saw the man that killed Pushmataha," I whispered.

"Where was he?" Joseph asked. "Was he hiding in the trees and watching the funeral?"

"Much worse than that, Joseph. He was leading the parade of soldiers. He was riding a white horse and wearing a fancy uniform. Everyone cheered him. The other soldiers did everything he told them to do."

"Yes, Andrew Jackson is more powerful than any soldier," Pushmataha said, as his ghost appeared between us. "Are you ready to go back with us, Joseph?"

"I am," Joseph said.

"Are you ready, Naomi?" Pushmataha asked.

"I am," Naomi said, stepping from behind the tree.

Naomi wore the scarf the women had woven to cover her short hair—a cruel reminder of when the Nahullo soldiers had taken Naomi, cut her long black hair, dressed her as a boy, and forced her to do their bidding.

Now, she once again wore a Choctaw dress.

Naomi was not a ghost, but she was strong and she was one of us.

"Will I have a chance to see this man on the white horse?" Joseph asked.

"Yes," Pushmataha said, "I want you to see him, but you must leave him alone."

"Why?"

"The past is done and cannot be undone. You, Naomi, and Isaac must understand this."

"Then why are we going?" Joseph asked.

"You cannot change the past, young Choctaws, but you can change the future," Pushmataha said. "And if you know the past, you can better change the future."

Chapter 5

Wagon of Death
Choctaw Nation, 1824

JOSEPH AND NAOMI had heard my description of traveling through time, but no one could be ready for their first journey backwards.

"Let's do this together," Pushmataha said. "Everyone take a breath."

We did, opening our mouths and sucking in a mouthful of air. "Wow!" we all said at the same time.

Our arms lifted, and we floated higher and higher, not fast like before, more like doves rising from the treetops.

"Is this how Isaac said it would be?" Pushmataha asked.

"Not exactly," Joseph said.

Pushmataha was at it again. *He's tricking them*, I thought, and I knew better than to say a word. I shook my head and glanced at the general. He smiled in reply.

"Maybe we should speed up a little," Pushmataha said.

With his words, the sun flashed before us like a giant boulder of fire. We covered our faces with our arms, but it didn't help. We sailed through the crackling flames. I bumped into Naomi, and we both collided with Joseph.

As suddenly as the fire appeared, it was gone. The darkness wrapped a chilly blanket of winter around us, which then melted into spring and summer. We spun so fast my ghost teeth left my mouth, and so did Joseph's and Naomi's. Seventy-twelve ghost teeth buzzing around our heads. What a sight!

I caught a glimpse of Pushmataha during a few seconds of daylight. He was not alone. He and a few hundred older Choctaw ghosts were munching what looked to be blackberries, as they sat on a soft white cloud watching us young ones swatting and grabbing our own teeth.

I opened my mouth to speak, but before I could say a word, two dozen teeth—my teeth—flew past my lips and rattled back into my mouth.

"Yuck!" I shouted and spit out my teeth. I tried talking, but without any teeth I couldn't make any sense.

"*Wheneral Cuthmashaha, pwease do sumtin,*" I sputtered.

The older Choctaw ghosts just laughed! Here I was, a very respectful almost eleven-year-old Choctaw ghost kid, and they were laughing at me.

"*Whop waffing, pwease,*" I said.

They only laughed harder.

"*Wheneral Cuthmashaha, pwease well whem I wham a whood kwid, pwease.*"

Hoke, if you think it's hard to read what a ghost kid says without his teeth, you should try talking without yours. Go ahead, try it. Turn to your best friend and try talking with your lips wrapped around your gums. Not so easy, is it? And you're not spinning around in the sky.

Suddenly, a star flashed by me like a tiny lightning bug, and everything slowed down, my mind and body both.

Hoke. What was I thinking? Of course they were laughing at me. That means they like me—and respect me. Choctaws are different in many ways, and this is one of them. When the elders respect you they play jokes on you, and if you don't get mad, you become one of them.

I closed my eyes and shut my mouth. When I opened them, the laughter was gone, my teeth had returned, and I was greeted with the most beautiful sunrise I had ever seen in my life—my living or my ghost life.

Maybe that is what Pushmataha is trying to teach me, I thought. *If I stop talking so much and instead look at what is around me, I can see beauty everywhere.*

Once more, I was with Naomi and Joseph. In silence we stared at the colors of the morning, the dark red edge to the clouds and the smiling yellow sun sitting on the shoulder of a hill to the east.

We floated over a road that cut through the thick forest below, as one lone wagon wound through the pine trees. Four horses, flapping their tails and stepping like the ponies in the funeral parade, pulled the wagon. Two uniformed soldiers drove the wagon.

I lifted my eyes for a brief moment and saw the faces of

Tim Tingle

Choctaw ghosts surrounding us. Most of them were old, like Pushmataha. Most of them had the same sad look on their faces that Pushmataha had worn in the graveyard.

"Something bad is about to happen," I whispered to my friends.

"You can feel it in the air," Naomi said, and Joseph nodded.

"The wagon was sent by General Jackson to take me to Washington," Pushmataha said.

Naomi and Joseph looked at him with surprise, but not me. I had already learned that General Pushmataha knew everything that was said or thought, now or before.

Hoke, maybe that is an exaggeration, but it's better to be on the safe side and assume he's always listening.

"Let's go closer," Pushmataha said. "Isaac, you can take your first ride on a fancy Nahullo wagon. Joseph and Naomi, I want you to stay out of sight for now."

Joseph knew what the general meant. Panther Joseph settled on a thick branch overlooking the road, while Naomi took shelter by the tree trunk.

"Don't let anyone see you," Pushmataha said, "but I want you to see everything that happens."

Naomi nodded and Panther Joseph flicked his tail in understanding.

Guess it's my turn, I thought.

Pushmataha smiled as I closed my eyes and floated into the wagon—where three plump Choctaw chiefs rolled back and forth with every bump in the rough road.

"I do not like riding in wagons!" the man sitting next to me hollered.

The booming voice sounded familiar, but I had to look at the chief's face to be sure who had spoken. Maybe you've already guessed who that chief was? Yes, our own General Pushmataha, Chief Pushmataha, sat complaining about the wagon ride. He looked twenty years younger than the Ghost Pushmataha I knew.

"I should have taken my own horse. I'd already be there!"

The other chiefs looked at each other without saying a word. *So I'm not the only Choctaw who keeps his mouth shut when Pushmataha is speaking*, I thought.

"Is it really that bad?" Ghost Pushmataha asked.

I slapped my hand over my mouth and Pushmataha smiled. The living Pushmataha did not know his own ghost was watching him, and that was a strange and new experience for me as well. For the first time in my life—my living or ghost life—I was watching a live person with his ghost.

Both spoke, but the living man could not hear the Ghost Pushmataha. I felt the shiver and knew something horrible was about to happen.

Time sped up, and the day passed in less than a minute. The wagon with the three Choctaw chiefs stopped, so the soldiers could cook a pot of stew over a campfire for the noon meal. Back on the wagon, the chiefs napped for the remainder of the day, till the sun grew pale and the dark of night surrounded us.

It was dinnertime. After tying the horses to a stout tree trunk, the soldiers cooked another pot of stew.

"Dried meat and beans," Pushmataha said. "Don't you men know how to cook anything else?"

"We are sorry, General," said one of the soldiers.

Yet, as he glanced at the other soldier, I saw them exchange a look of disrespect. *These soldiers are like the soldiers that burned our houses down,* I thought. *They are pretending to take orders from Pushmataha, but someone else sent them here. They are here for a reason Pushmataha does not suspect.*

Suddenly I knew. "Andrew Jackson," I whispered. "These soldiers are under the orders of Andrew Jackson."

"You are a smart young man, Isaac," Pushmataha said. "That's why I wanted you to see my funeral, so you could understand why you lost your homes."

"Why so many Choctaws died," I said.

"Yes, and why the dying continues."

For the first time since the time travels began, I wanted to be with my family. I wanted to make sure my brother, Luke, and my mother and father were safe. I wanted to make sure Jumper was getting enough to eat.

"It's the least I can do," Pushmataha said.

With a quick shiver, I found myself floating over the campfire of my family. Jumper sat close to the fire, licking his paws after a supper of squirrel meat. Little ghost Nita sat by her mother and father. Her mother still looked sad, as a mother who has lost a child is wont to do. I knew I only had a short time, so I floated to the ground. I was about to sit down next to my mother when I heard the rattling.

Whirrrrr, whirrrr.

"Halito, Stella," I said, and Rattlesnake Stella *whirrrred* a greeting.

"Look what they are eating," Pushmataha said, pointing to the cooking bowl. "Choctaw pashofa, corn soup. Be nice if I could have a bowl of pashofa on my last trip to Washington."

The corn soup looked so thick I could almost taste it, but ghosts can't taste anything, so looking will have to do.

"We can't taste food, but we can time travel, Isaac. Hoke, say hello to your family," Pushmataha said.

I closed my eyes and floated into sight, standing by the cooking fire. At first they didn't see me. The night fog was thick, and soft snowflakes filled the air and covered the ground. Everything was white.

My father leaned over the fire with his arms spread wide, to keep the snow from melting and putting out the flames. My mother reached from under her blanket and stirred the pashofa with a long wooden spoon. Nita's mother and father wrapped their blankets tighter and huddled closer to the fire.

Jumper was the first to see me. My funny dog barked and ran around and around the fire till everyone lifted their heads from their blankets.

"Isaac," my father said.

"Oh son, how are you?" asked my mother.

"He looks hoke to me," said Jumper, wagging his tail and dancing around the fire.

Nita's mother and father sat up and looked around.

"Nita is here, too," I said to them.

Nita giggled her sweet little girl laugh and appeared to her parents. Her mother buried her face in her blanket and sobbed.

"I am hoke, Mother," Nita said.

"Yes, you are, my pretty Nita," her father said.

The three hugged in such a tight and tender circle that I wished Nita were still alive and with her family.

"Where is Naomi?" her father asked.

"Your older daughter is strong and well," Pushmataha answered, appearing before the fire. "I will see that she returns to you soon. Now, Isaac and I must go."

"Chipisha latchiki," everyone said. "See you later."

Chapter 6

A Chip Off the Old Stone

OUR RETURN trip to 1824 was a quick flight through a starry sky. I knew serious things were about to happen, for Pushmataha had no time for tricks—no fiery suns or sudden darkness this time. We left the freezing trail and soon found ourselves over the wagon of the Choctaw chiefs.

I looked for Joseph and Naomi, and Pushmataha, reading my thoughts, pointed to the top of the wagon. I floated higher to get a better view. I saw only three large chests, filled with clothing, shoes, and whatever the chiefs might need in the Nahullo capital of Washington.

I floated closer and finally spotted my friends, snuggled and hidden between the chests. Panther Joseph was curled in a half-moon around Naomi, who slept with her head on his furry black shoulders.

"They are safe till daylight," Pushmataha said. "Now, Isaac, let's look inside."

We leaned toward the windows and he pointed at the three sleeping Choctaw chiefs.

"That is Chief Puckshenubbe, from the Northern District," he said, pointing to the youngest of the three. "And the older man, Chief Moshulatubbee, is from the Central District. He is a sweet old man, but General Jackson is not afraid of him. Chief Moshulatubbee is too old to cause anyone any trouble. The handsome one you have already met. That is yours truly only a few years ago."

I smiled. Even as the wagon carried him to his death, Pushmataha had time for a little humor. I was beginning to love this Choctaw general, almost like a second father.

"That is me before the coffin and the funeral, before my days of waiting."

"Waiting for what?" I asked.

"For General Jackson to see me. He tried to move us from our homes years ago. I made a trip to what was supposed to be our new home. I liked our old one better. We are Choctaws, people of the woods and rivers. The new land was dry and rocky. I told him we would not move.

"He invited me to Washington to talk about it. He even sent this wagon to make sure I came when he wanted, but he never had time for our meeting. For almost a month, I waited in the Nahullo capital city. I had no friends there, and I grew very sick, Isaac."

Pushmataha hung his head and said nothing for a moment or two. I had seen the sadness on his face at the cemetery, and now it came again. General Pushmataha, powerful Pushmataha, was sharing something about himself he never shared with anyone—but only for a moment.

"We are jumping too far ahead," he said. "I want you to first see what happened on our trip."

A dark cloud passed over the moon, as if he had made it happen. Chief Puckshenubbe lifted his head from his chest, rubbed his eyes, and poked his head through the window.

"Halito!" he shouted, banging his fist on the wagon roof. "Hello up there. Can you hear me?"

"What is it?" hollered the young soldier driving the wagon. "What do you want?"

"I have some business to attend to in the woods," Puckshenubbe replied, "and it cannot wait."

"Whoa," the young driver said.

He tugged on the reins and the horses came to a stop. Then he paused. He didn't leap from the wagon and open the door for Chief Puckshenubbe. Instead, he looked over his shoulder, as if he had a secret.

He leaned in to the older soldier and whispered, "Is this a good place, Sergeant Hill? Do you know these woods?"

"It could work," Sergeant Hill said. "We'll have to drag his body and toss it over the cliff, but it's just around the next curve. I'll need your help, Corporal Angel."

I looked to Pushmataha. *Drag his body*, I thought, and Pushmataha nodded.

He blames himself, I thought.

"I should blame myself, Isaac," the general said. "It was

43

my fault. Chief Puckshenubbe has a sweet wife and three little girls, and he is gone from their lives forever. He is on this wagon because of me. Andrew Jackson invited him to come with me."

"Here, let me help you," Corporal Angel said, opening the door and reaching for Chief Puckshenubbe's closest arm.

"I am fine, or will be in a minute," Chief Puckshenubbe said. The chief stepped from the wagon and entered the woods, as the corporal peered through the window, making sure the other two chiefs were asleep.

"I wasn't sleeping," Pushmataha said. "I had my eyes closed, but I was not asleep. I should have gone with my friend to be safe. But I trusted them. I trusted him!"

The young corporal quietly closed the door and leaned against the wagon, as if he were simply waiting for the chief's return. But Sergeant Hill did not wait. He hopped from the wagon and slipped into the woods, following Chief Puckshenubbe.

I followed them both.

I saw the sergeant pick up a sharp stone the size of a man's boot. Chief Puckshenubbe leaned against a tree in the shadows of the thick forest. His back was to us. The sergeant crept up close behind him, stopping every few steps and looking over his shoulders, first one and then the other.

Why is he doing that? I thought. *He knows no one else is there.*

"Guilt," Pushmataha answered. "He is guilty for what he is about to do."

I heard the crackle of leaves as someone, a living someone, joined us.

The sergeant knelt. He had heard the footsteps, too.

I turned to see Joseph, Panther Joseph. His coat was so black and the night so dark, he was unseen by the soldier with the stone. With slow and careful placing of each paw to the ground, Joseph stepped closer and closer to the sergeant. As Sergeant Hill raised the stone to strike Chief Puckshenubbe, Joseph leapt.

"Yes!" I whisper-shouted. "Don't let him kill our Choctaw chief!"

Panther Joseph reached the sergeant just before the edge of the stone struck the head of Chief Puckshenubbe. The panther's jaws were wide open, and his long, sharp teeth flashed in the moonlight. Panther Joseph snapped his jaws shut on the arm of the sergeant.

I expected a gush of blood from Sergeant Hill's wrist. I expected him to drop the stone and roll to the ground, fighting off the panther. I expected to see the sergeant lying limp and lifeless on the forest floor. But none of that happened.

Instead, Joseph flew through the sergeant as if he were a ghost. He sailed through the tree trunk and landed twenty feet away in a bramble of bushes. The stone struck Chief Puckshenubbe and he crumpled to the ground. His hands flew to the back of his head, his knees buckled, and his body went limp.

"Ooooooh," he moaned, as the darkness sucked the life from him.

The sergeant dropped the stone and dashed back to the wagon. The stone dripped with the still wet blood of our Choctaw chief. I rushed to the chief's side as Joseph returned to his human self and knelt to join me. I slowly lifted Chief Puckshenubbe's head.

His eyes were open but unseeing, staring off into the distance. I placed my ear to his chest, as I had seen my father do, but his heart was silent.

"You cannot change the past," Pushmataha whispered.

We stood up and stepped away from the body.

"What should we do?" I asked. "We can't leave him here."

"The soldiers plan to throw his body over a nearby cliff," said Pushmataha.

"Can we stop them?" Joseph asked.

"No, Joseph. And do you know why?"

I glanced at Joseph, and he turned to look at me.

"We cannot change the past," we said together.

"His body will be taken care of," Pushmataha said. "The Choctaw women are stronger than the soldiers. They'll make sure of it."

"How will they know?" I asked, and then felt foolish. Choctaw women, ghosts or living, know everything.

Chief Pushmataha didn't bother to answer. He picked up the bloodied stone and smashed it against a rock jutting from a tree root. He picked up two pieces spotted with blood.

"Here, young man," he said, handing one chip of the stone to Joseph. "May you never forget what you saw this day. May you work for the good, so this will never happen again."

"I will work for the good for the rest of my life," said Joseph.

Chapter 7
Trip to Washington

"HURRY," THE SERGEANT said to the corporal, "before the others wake up. I need your help."

"What is it?" Pushmataha asked from inside the wagon.

"Nothing," said the sergeant. "We're taking a break; that's all. If any of you want to stretch your legs, now is the time."

Chief Moshulatubbee still slept.

"Stretch your own legs," said Pushmataha. "I'm going back to sleep." He wrapped a thick blanket around his shoulders and his head fell to his chest. He was soon snoring.

I looked over at my friend, at Ghost Pushmataha.

He was biting his lip and shaking his head. "If only I had followed them through the woods," he said. "I could not have brought General Puckshenubbe back to life, but I would have known General Jackson could not be trusted. I could have saved so many Choctaws from death, from the fires, from the freezing cold."

Tears rolled down his cheeks and I put my hand on his shoulder. Hoke, I am still a kid, but when a grown-up needs comforting, you have to try. "General Pushmataha?"

"Yes, Isaac."

"We are your soldiers, Joseph and Naomi and I."

"And so am I, General. If you will have me."

We looked up in surprise at this new voice. Before us stood the ghost of General Puckshenubbe, with his head bowed.

"General Puckshenubbe," said Pushmataha. "Halito, my friend. I have missed you so. Where have you been?"

"I followed my body around for who knows how long," he said, "but, as you know, family comes first. I now spend most of my time with my wife. I didn't want to scare our children, but they now know I am a ghost and that I'm there when they need me."

"It's hard for our families to know we're still alive," I said.

The two generals turned and stared at me. No one said a word, but I knew what both were thinking. This was a talk between generals, and I should be listening, not talking.

"I am sorry," I said quietly.

"That's hoke, Isaac," General Puckshenubbe said. A big smile spread across his face. "I have been watching you awhile. Your talking comes as no surprise to me."

Then these two ghost Choctaw generals, both killed by soldiers they had trusted, erupted in the biggest belly laugh I have ever heard from the living or the dead. They grabbed their bellies and laughed till the leaves shook and shivered and fell from the trees. And they were still laughing when Joseph and Naomi joined us. We waited for their laughter to fizzle, and by human time, this took maybe ten minutes. By ghost time, I'd say a few centuries, or so it seemed. Naomi was the first to step forward when the laughter stopped. With bowed head, she stopped five steps from the general.

"My name is Naomi," she said softly.

"I am Joseph," my panther friend said, standing beside her.

"I am very honored to meet you both," said General Puckshenubbe. "I have traveled forward in time, to your days on the Trail. You are both fine Choctaws. I am proud to know you."

"Yakoke," Naomi and Joseph said together.

"And young Isaac," General Puckshenubbe added, "I am proud to know you as well. Please do not take my laughter wrong."

"If I have learned anything from General Pushmataha, it's that when you're Choctaw laughter never sleeps," I said.

Everyone nodded and smiled.

"Hoke," said Pushmataha. "I want the young ones to see what they did to you, General Puckshenubbe."

"I understand," said Puckshenubbe. "Do you mind if I don't go? I've seen it too many times already."

Pushmataha gave his old friend a tight hug. "Chipisha latchiki," he said, and then General Pushmataha turned to us. "Naomi and Joseph, try not to make a sound."

My friends nodded and we set out. We followed the soldiers to the edge of the woods, to Chief Puckshenubbe's body.

"It's done," the sergeant said. "He's dead. One down, one to go, but that is Jackson's business. Our job is to get the body to the cliff before the others know what happened."

"Then what?"

"We wait till somebody wants to know what's taking so long. Then we go looking for the dead Choctaw and start hollering, like his falling from the cliff was an accident. Those dumb redskins will believe it."

I didn't have to look at Chief Pushmataha to know what he was feeling. His sadness filled the air. We stood by—unable to do anything as the soldiers dragged Chief Puckshenubbe's body, still dripping with blood from the wound on the back of his head. Each soldier took an arm as they dragged him over the rocky forest floor, over fallen trees and through thick bramble bushes, carving a bloody path through the night forest.

I glanced at Naomi and saw tears flowing down her cheeks, but when I looked at Joseph, my jaw dropped. He was standing tall on the legs of the panther, but he still wore his clothes. Sharp claws stuck through the sleeves of his shirt and silky black panther hairs rose from his collar.

I had never seen Joseph this way, ever, and I knew he was going through some strange and difficult choice.

Maybe what he saw was so evil that he did not want to be human anymore. Maybe he was thinking about leaving his friends, his Choctaw life, and running away to the forest.

"No, Joseph," I said. "I need you. We need you. Naomi would still be with the soldiers if you hadn't helped her escape. Please stay with us."

Joseph tilted his head and looked at me as if he were seeing me for the first time. He blinked as he stared first at the wagon, then at the road, and finally deep into the forest, as if discovering where and who he was.

Bowing his head, he slowly lifted his palms and ran them from his forehead to the back of his neck, wrapping his fingers around the panther fur. In that motion, Joseph became the panther. He leapt to a nearby tree and was gone, following the soldiers and the body.

Those of us who remained floated slower than ever, so Naomi could keep up and so we could listen to the soldiers' conversation.

"Maybe this wasn't such a good idea after all," said Sergeant Hill, mopping his brow as he rested on a fallen tree trunk. "I don't know why we have to do all this sneaking around. We should just shoot all three of 'em and toss the bodies over the cliff. Nobody's gonna care. They'll be dead soon anyway."

"But didn't you say General Jackson had a plan?" the corporal asked.

"Oh yes," said Sergeant Hill, "we have to treat these Indians with dignity and respect. Remember, he is now Senator Jackson, and that's what he wants. Dignity and respect, 'for Pushmataha especially,' he told me. And why? So he can kill Pushmataha, that's the real reason."

"I don't understand," the corporal said.

"We're not supposed to understand. Our job is to do the dirty work, to do what they order us to do, nothing more, nothing less."

"But why?"

"So nobody knows that our Senator Jackson, our hero, plans on murdering one of his fellow officers."

"He can't keep that a secret!"

"You think not? Oh, maybe not forever. Maybe someday, somebody will begin to suspect this was all part of a big plan. Maybe. In two hundred years, when we're all dead and gone."

As his words floated through the air, time froze. A loud clap of thunder shook the world, followed by streaks of lightning, scratching the night sky with sharp, bitter nails. Balls of fire exploded, raining down debris, rattling the leaves and treetops and leaving nothing untouched.

I expected the soldiers to run for cover, maybe to be struck by a fireball, but they didn't move.

"This fiery sky is for our eyes only," Pushmataha said. "Our ancestors are angered by the sergeant's words and the senator's plans. No one is so powerful he can slay so many and go unpunished."

"No," I whispered. "We know, we Choctaws know, and we will not let the truth stay buried, not in a cemetery and not over the edge of a cliff."

"That is why I chose you, Son," Chief Pushmataha

said, putting his arm around my shoulder.

He had called me Son. I closed my eyes and felt strong and good. Not happy, not while staring at the lifeless body of a Choctaw chief, but I felt strong.

"We cannot change the past, but we can let others know," Joseph said.

"Yakoke, thank you for including me," Naomi said. "I will be careful, and I will never let the truth stay hidden."

We stood as one—Joseph and I, Naomi, and our leader Chief Pushmataha—together in our Choctaw purpose.

Chapter 8
What to Believe?

WE WATCHED THE soldiers drag Chief Puckshenubbe over the rough ground, leaving a long trail of blood behind them. We soon stood in the moonlight, overlooking a deep gorge lined with trees and boulders.

"He will never make it to the bottom," I whispered.

"That is why Puckshenubbe does not want to watch," Pushmataha said.

We stood in silence as the soldiers picked up the body, Sergeant Hill holding the arms and the corporal his ankles, preparing to swing Chief Puckshenubbe's corpse over the cliff.

"Ready," said the sergeant. "One, two, three!"

Chief Puckshenubbe was a heavy man, in life and death, and the soldiers were only able to fling his body a few feet over the cliff's edge. I covered my eyes with my hands but could not stop myself from watching. As I peeped through my fingers, I saw—and heard—the true miracle of the day.

The first sound was of bones breaking, as Puckshenubbe fell. Each time his body hit the rocks, the bone-breaking sound continued.

Then came the miracle. The moonlight grew brighter, then brighter still, as a silvery beam shone on the scene below us. A soft hum of singing blew on the wind, and in that breeze, we heard a song—an old Choctaw song.

> *Hinauchi pasali*
> *Bok chitto anaali*
> *Yayali, Yayali*

As we leaned over the edge of the cliff, we saw a gathering of Choctaw women ghosts, too many to count, and as they flew in one after another, time slowed to a crawl.

I had experienced this slowing down of time often since Pushmataha had first taken me from the Trail of Walking People, but never before like this.

The Choctaw women were of all ages, from tiny girls as young as Nita to older women with gray hair and skinny arms. They circled Chief Puckshenubbe; they flew in and out of his falling body; they eased him from one rock to the next on his downward fall; and they finally settled him on a thick tree trunk, reaching out from the side of the cliff like a strong man's arm. The chief's body draped over the tree, and his long hair waved in the cool night breeze. The song continued as Chief Puckshenubbe's body swayed over the gorge.

"I wish he could see this," I whispered. "I wish the chief could see what the Choctaw women have done to soften his death fall."

"The women are here for you, Isaac, you and your friends. They did not want you to remember the cruelty, the blood, the broken bones, the disrespect for the passage to another life."

"Why?" Naomi asked.

"They want you young Choctaws to one day be able to forgive. That is what can save us as a people. We must always forgive," said Chief Pushmataha.

*****

We retraced our steps to the wagon, down the path washed with our chief's blood. We walked in silence, and the moonlight sighed and settled into midnight.

That's when Chief Puckshenubbe joined us again.

"I saw," he said. "I tried to stay away but could not. I heard the song and felt the arms of the women, cradling my body from the fall. It will be easier now. Knowing makes it easier."

"I hope someday I can be as good and strong as the women we saw," Naomi said.

We menfolk, all four of us, did not say a word, did not even glance at each other. We didn't have to. We all shared the same thought. *You already are, Naomi.* A shout brought us back to the present—or what passed for the present in our time-traveling adventure.

"Time to move!" shouted Sergeant Hill, poking his head inside the wagon.

"Took you all long enough," Chief Pushmataha said.

"Not our fault," the sergeant said. "We fell asleep waiting for your chief friend to return. Is he back and in the wagon?"

"No," said Pushmataha. "We thought he was with you."

The corporal flung the wagon door open. "He's not here?" he asked. "Where is he?"

Chief Pushmataha and Chief Moshulatubbee climbed from the wagon and stretched.

"He can't be far," said Pushmataha. "There's no reason to wander, and he doesn't know these woods."

"Maybe something happened to him," said the sergeant. "There is a cliff not far from here."

"Our friend has never been one to take chances, not Puckshenubbe," said Pushmataha. "Which way did he go?"

"That way," said the corporal. "We waited for him for a while, and when he didn't return, we climbed back on the wagon and fell asleep."

"Follow me," the sergeant said, "and stay together."

Once more we made the trip through the woods to the cliff, trailing after the murdering soldiers. Naomi dashed from one tree to the next, careful not to be seen, while Panther Joseph stayed on the overhead tree limbs in case the soldiers spotted Naomi and she needed help.

"General!" yelled the sergeant. "Did you lose your way?" Over and over he shouted his lie.

The living Chief Pushmataha now seemed quite alert, studying the ground and brush for any sign of his friend. I saw in his eyes the Pushmataha I knew, a friendly old man much smarter than he seemed. The soldiers led the two Choctaw chiefs away from the tree where their peer had been murdered, in an effort to make sure neither saw the bloody stone weapon.

But Pushmataha remembered where he had last seen Puckshenubbe enter the woods, and he quietly slipped away in that direction. He soon came to a halt and stepped back in horror. Blood splattered the ground where Puckshenubbe had been killed.

I expected Pushmataha to shout, to call the others over. But Pushmataha was too smart for that. Instead, he hurried to the soldiers, limping as he walked.

"Hold up," he said. "Please, wait. It seems I have lost the heel to my boot. I'm going to the wagon for another pair. It won't take me long." Without waiting for an answer or permission, Pushmataha limped away. As soon as he was out of sight of the soldiers, he began to run. When he reached the wagon, he did not bother to change his boots. Instead he found a pistol, made certain it was loaded, and tucked it into his belt at his back. He soon caught up with the others.

"Hoke," Pushmataha said. "Sorry to keep you waiting."

"You didn't see any sign of your friend, did you?" asked the sergeant.

"No, I didn't see a thing," Pushmataha lied.

He is doing everything he can to stay alive, to keep the other chief and himself from being murdered, too, I thought.

By now the soldiers were tired of the game, of playing the lie. They walked faster, without bothering to look or call out to Puckshenubbe as they hurried to the cliff.

"I hope he didn't come this way," the sergeant said, stepping from the woods to the cliff's edge. A cloud covered the moon for a brief moment and darkness fell upon us.

When a beam of light shone from the sky to the floor of the gorge, Pushmataha pointed to the chief's body without saying a word.

"He must have stumbled around until he fell," Sergeant Hill said.

Pushmataha said not a word, but grabbed Chief Moshulatubbee by the shoulder and led him away from the soldiers. *He's making sure the soldiers don't push them off the cliff,* I thought.

"We must retrieve his body," Pushmataha said.

"We don't have time for that," the sergeant said. "Besides, it would be too dangerous. We'll stop at the next town and let the authorities know where he is. They'll hold the body until the Choctaws can come pick it up, unless you want them to bury it here?"

"He is not an *it*," said Pushmataha. "He is our friend and a Choctaw chief. He is Chief Puckshenubbe."

"I'm sorry if I was disrespectful," said the sergeant, turning away to hide the impolite look on his face. "We've got to go. Let's get back to the wagon."

As the two remaining Choctaw chiefs and the soldiers returned to the wagon, Ghost Pushmataha gathered us together. "We will be leaving soon for Washington, the capital town. To understand what you will see there, you had to see how Chief Puckshenubbe died."

"You had your pistol," Joseph said. "Why didn't you kill the soldiers for what they did?"

Naomi and I looked hard at him.

"I'm sorry," he said. "Forgive me, Chief Pushmataha. I meant no disrespect. I'm angry, that's all."

"You have a right to be, Joseph. We are all angry, but killing those men would make me a criminal. I'd die before a firing squad," said Pushmataha. "And I still had a job to do."

"You wanted to stop the burning of our houses," I said. "You wanted to save our homes."

"That was my hope. I made many mistakes, my young friends," he said, "but maybe you won't make the same ones."

Chapter 9

Choctaw Heaven

"MAY I ASK A question?" Naomi said.

Chief Pushmataha did not need to look at me. I knew what he was thinking. *Young Isaac, do you see how your friend addresses me? She does not blurt out a comment. She asks permission.* He turned to me and nodded, letting me know I had read him right.

"Of course, Naomi. What is it?" he said.

"How long have we been here, in real time?"

"You want to know about your family, don't you?"

"Yes. May I see them again?"

Joseph and I leaned forward, and Pushmataha saw the eager looks on our faces.

"I am proud of all three of you for never forgetting your families," Pushmataha said. "Hoke, let's go."

Pushmataha appeared to be the most powerful ghost in the world—either world. He gave us a fluffy round cloud to sit upon, and then he floated the cloud over the cliff and into a beam of moonlight. The cloud, lifting us with it, slowly rose into the night sky.

When we looked down into the gorge at the body of Chief Puckshenubbe, four Choctaw ghost women were singing over him, waving sticks of burning cedar. Even from far away, we could lift our heads and take in deep breaths of the sweet smell.

I can't taste food, but I can at least smell cedar, I thought.

Soon the aroma of cedar surrounded us, and we started spinning, slowly at first, then faster as the sun rose and set, many times. Finally we found ourselves above a long road twisting through the Mississippi woods.

"Morning is the best time of the day," said Chief Pushmataha. "I will leave you now. I would like to spend time with my own family. But if you need me, I'll be there for you, always know that."

Our cedar cloud floated down and settled into a small clearing of cottonwoods. My family sat by the road, wrapped in blankets and nestled close to a campfire. Months ago, when our town was burned and we first started the long walk, we were two families, two separate families. But now we were one. Naomi and her parents, Ruth and Gabe. My mother, father, and big brother Luke, and, of course, Nita.

Nita noticed us first, which made sense since she is the little sister ghost of Naomi and she loved her sister as only a child can love, with giggles and smiles and sloppy girl kisses.

"I would have seen you first, but I was busy guarding the campsite," Jumper said, stepping into the woods.

I laughed long and loud at that one. "You were eating breakfast and didn't want to be bothered, Jumper," I said.

"So can you blame me?" Jumper replied. "Not everybody can fly when they want to get somewhere. Some of us have to walk. Ever heard of that?"

"I have missed you so much, Jumper!"

Jumper smiled his best puppy-dog-smile. "Me, too," he admitted, wagging his tail.

Soon we were all gathered around the morning fire. Naomi sat between her mother and father, with little ghost Nita in her lap. Her mother always kept Nita's body close, rolled up in a blanket by her side.

"I am not going to cry," her mother said, brushing the tears from her cheeks, "but I am so happy to see you. You look well."

"I am fine," Naomi said, "and I missed you, too. How have you been?"

"Cold. The snow was so thick yesterday we could barely see the road, but don't worry about us."

"Ask her about the cut on her head," Nita said.

"Shhh! Naomi doesn't need to know about that."

Naomi's brow wrinkled as she touched her mother's cheek.

"I'm sorry, Mother. I wish I could have been here for you."

"She slipped and fell on an icy patch in the road," her father said. He pulled the hair away from her neck, revealing a deep cut, coated in dried blood.

"It doesn't hurt, not anymore. Alikchi Stella cooked an herb brew and made it better."

Oh no, I thought. *I forgot about Stella.*

Stella must have heard her name mentioned.

Whrrrr. Whrrrr.

Rattlesnake Stella slithered from under a flat rock and wrapped herself around my ankle. "Nice to see you, too, Isaac," she said, and then just as suddenly as she appeared she was gone. I felt two hands touch my shoulders from behind.

"It's me," Stella said, joining us by the fire. "The me you know best."

My gaze circled the faces of family members and stopped at the face of my brother. Luke was staring at me and nodding his head in pride. I lifted my hand and gave him a small wave. We were brothers and had been through so much together; we did not need to shower each other with affection. We knew how we felt.

In many ways, I have it easy. I'm never hungry or sleepy. I never feel pain. Luke does, but he can't show it. He's too busy watching out for my parents, too busy making sure they don't worry about him.

I saw something in that moment by the campfire with my family—something I had never seen before. Luke had become like a father since I had become a ghost.

Chapter 10

Panther Returns

"TIME TO WALK!" shouted the soldier. "Put out the fires and get moving!"

Stella stood and tossed handfuls of snow on the fire until the embers fizzled and died. Naomi washed the clay dishes with melted snow while the mothers brushed icicles from the blankets.

The soldier snapped the reins of his horse and turned to go, when he spotted Naomi.

"You don't look sick," he said, climbing from the saddle and approaching her.

"I feel much better now," Naomi said.

She had smartly figured out that her parents must have claimed she was ill when she went missing the few days.

"Your father said you were with those old ladies, the bonepickers. I think I'd rather die than spend a day in their wagon," the soldier said. "What was it like?"

Naomi was becoming nervous, I could tell, and so could the soldier. He circled her and leaned close, too close for a Nahullo man talking to a young Choctaw woman.

"You're not lying to me, are you?"

Naomi turned her head away from him and covered her face with her arms. "Please leave me alone," she said.

I knew what was tormenting Naomi, and it wasn't the pesky soldier. She was surrounded by memories, memories of the soldiers when she was forced to live with them, when she had to cook and serve and spend every waking hour in the clutches of the meanest soldier I had ever met—Leader.

"What's going on?"

A strong voice cut through the morning air.

Speak of the devil, it was Leader himself. He rode roughshod into our camp.

"No trouble here," my father said. "We're almost ready to walk."

"I saw the girl who's been sick and was welcoming her back," the soldier said. "But she won't talk about what it was like in the bonepickers' wagon."

Leader looked at Naomi and smiled, but his smile was dark and angry. "Thank you for your help," he said to the soldier. "I'll take over from here."

"Yes, sir," the soldier said, saluting Leader and mounting his horse.

Our families quickly stepped to the road to begin the long day's walk, only to be greeted with a thick flurry of snow. Luke hurried from one person to the next, covering their faces with blankets and pointing them in the right direction. "Step careful and move slow," he said. "This will be over soon."

I shook my head and laughed, not a funny ha-ha laugh but a laugh of pride and amazement. Luke was becoming a father, not just to my family but to everyone around him.

Not too long ago, it had fallen to me to do all the chores, not just my share, but all the chores, so Luke could spend his days playing stickball with his friends. I could still recall Mother hollering for us from the front porch, with something she needed us to do. For Luke, that call was his signal to run off, leaving me to tote the water or collect the firewood.

Now I laughed so loud at the sight of my brother being a helper that I had to turn away and cover my mouth.

"Don't let him hear you laugh," said Stella, laughing a little herself at the brotherly role reversal.

We had expected Leader to ride away once he saw we were all on the road and walking, but he lingered. And he rode his horse close behind Naomi. She tried to step aside and let him pass, but his intent was never to pass her by. He reined his horse closer and closer, and Naomi walked faster and faster, slipping on the icy road and struggling to keep her balance.

Leader smiled at her obvious unease. His was a strange and deathly race that everyone saw but no one could stop.

No one, that is, but Joseph. I knew Joseph was hiding nearby. I had seen Panther Joseph crouching in a tree near the road when we began to walk—and then high on a rock outcropping. Joseph had risked his life more than once to save Naomi, and I knew he would never allow Leader to harm her. Another quick survey of the area found Panther Joseph now in a tall oak, and I watched in fear as he backed down the trunk of the tree and began to stalk Leader and his horse. The snow swirled like tiny gnats, so thick that Leader never saw the panther coming.

"I'm here if you need me," Leader said, pulling up close to Naomi. He reached out and touched her neck. Naomi jumped.

Panther Joseph had drawn closer as well, and he reared onto his hind legs and flashed his sharp teeth. With his paws drawn in so he wouldn't leave a scar, he swatted Leader's horse on the flanks. The horse bucked and tossed his rider to the ground. Leader rolled to his feet, drew his pistol, and fired into the air.

"Halt!" he shouted. "Everyone halt!"

Up and down the line, the other soldiers shouted, "Halt! Stay where you are!"

Choctaw walkers froze in their tracks and waited. A captain rode to the sound of the gunfire and drew his horse to a stop when he spotted Leader.

"I will wait for your orders, General," he said, saluting.

"Stand at attention," Leader said. "One of these Choctaws scared my horse and tried to kill me. I intend to find out who and punish him accordingly."

I shivered at his words. Luke wrapped his arms around our father and mother. Naomi moved to her parents, and Nita clutched her mother's legs tight. One thing was certain. Once Leader claimed that someone had tried to kill him, he would take his revenge only in the death of one of us.

"What can I do to help, sir?" the captain asked.

"Stand everyone from this campsite before me."

The soldier hurried to obey, shoving both families into a single row, facing Leader.

"Remove their blankets," Leader barked.

Once again the soldier followed orders, yanking blankets from people's backs and piling them at Leader's feet.

"Now," said Leader, "we wait. The guilty party will either come forward and confess his crime or watch like a coward while his family and the others freeze to death in the snow."

The captain stared ahead, not knowing what to say.

"Start a fire and make me some coffee."

"Yes, sir."

The snow by now was a mix of icy sleet, and it fell harder than before. I saw that my mother was thinner than I remembered. Her wrists poked from her dress like skinny branches, and she shivered, a small tree in a cold, cruel wind. She stood between Luke and my father, and I saw Luke reach around her to grip my father's hand, a silent gesture of strength unseen by the Nahullos.

Naomi stood tall, flanked by her mother and father. Sharp threads of sleet slapped her face, and she buried her face in her hands. Little ghost Nita could not be still. She moved through the legs of her mother, sat on the shoulders of her father, touched the hands of her sister, and kissed the cheeks of every member of both families.

"What did you two troublemakers do?" a soft voice whispered in my ear.

I turned to see the ghost of Pushmataha, shaking his head as he took in the scene before him.

"Hoke, let's move to the woods so we can talk."

Chapter 11
Death by Sword

WE JOINED JOSEPH IN A circle of pine trees far
enough from the Trail that we could not be overheard.

"It was my fault," said Joseph. "Leader rode his horse
too close to Naomi. He was teasing her, and she was
afraid—I was afraid—of what he might do. He hurt her
before, and I wasn't going to let him do it again."

Chief Pushmataha listened in silence. When Joseph
finished, he looked through the trees at the Choctaw families standing in the sleet, without blankets. He cast his
gaze to the ground before replying. He was such a great
man, Pushmataha. He taught us his lesson without ever
saying a word. By looking at the result of Joseph's actions,
six Choctaws shivering in the snow, he forced us to see
how Joseph had put all of us in serious danger.

"I am sorry," Joseph said. "I was not thinking."

"We cannot change the past," Pushmataha reminded us. "Let us watch for now. We will soon know what to do."

We hid behind a thick clump of bushes, now also covered in snow, while Leader pranced his horse up and down the line, sipping his coffee and growing visibly impatient.

"I will wait all day until somebody points to the guilty party," Leader said. "Better yet, the person who tried to knock me to the ground should confess."

Joseph rose to step forward, but Pushmataha grabbed him by the shoulder. He held a hand in the air, a signal to be patient.

I looked at my father and could almost see his muscles twitching to respond. I knew he would give his life before he would let anyone else die. My mother must have thought the same thing, for I saw her tighten the grip on his arm.

Everyone knew it was the panther that had jumped at Leader's horse, and I knew their eyes were scanning the edges of the forest, looking for Joseph.

In her family, Naomi was the strong one, and I knew she would give her life before she would give up Joseph. Still, I would never have guessed what happened next.

"I did it," Naomi's mother said, stepping forward. "I saw you following Naomi, and I knocked you from your horse."

"She did not," Naomi said. "Mother is trying to protect me. I kicked the leg of your horse and made you fall."

"Leader, I will not let the women of my family lie to protect me," Naomi's father said, stepping in front of his wife and daughter.

"Please stop it!" Luke shouted. "Naomi is my friend, and you all know that it was me who knocked Leader from his horse."

"Chahta sia hoke," Pushmataha said. "I am so proud to be Choctaw."

We all felt proud that our kinfolks were each and every one willing to offer up their life to save another.

Where there is one wolf, there is another, I thought.

"Yes, young Isaac, once again you are right."

"I didn't say anything."

"I heard you, too," said Joseph. "But what does it mean?"

We both looked at Chief Pushmataha. The thought must have come from his strange and wise old mind.

Pushmataha smiled and shrugged, pointing a thumb over his shoulder. A large male wolf, his den now filled with snow, was climbing a boulder that jutted over the road. When he spotted the shivering Choctaws, the wolf bared his teeth and growled, a low and terrifying growl. I was reminded of the wolf that had claimed my life so long ago.

What more could go wrong? Once more, I felt the pain of the wolf's teeth sinking into my throat and my shirt wet with my own blood. Pushmataha put his arm on my shoulder and waved a finger in front of my face. *Just wait*, he seemed to be saying.

Joseph, however, could not wait. "I did it," Joseph said, stepping from the bushes and approaching Leader. "You all know I did it."

Leader smiled and nodded. "This is far better than I could imagine, young man," he said. "You've been a hard one to find."

Joseph said nothing.

"So what sort of magic are you planning now?" Leader asked. At the sight of Joseph, a dozen soldiers rode to the general's aid, their rifles pointed at the young Choctaw troublemaker.

"I am here to take my punishment," Joseph said. "Please do not hurt anyone else."

"Kneel," Leader commanded.

Joseph turned to look at his friends for the last time as a living Choctaw, and then knelt before Leader and bowed his head.

"Aren't you forgetting?" Naomi said, and everyone turned to her. "General, you are alive today because of him. He could have left you to the wolf, but he risked his life for you."

Leader hesitated, only for an instant, but that instant was enough. His soldiers put down their weapons and waited for new orders. Leader pulled a sword from his saddle and walked to the kneeling Joseph.

"Don't move, son," he said. "If you don't want your friends to die, do not move."

Leader gripped his sword with both hands and moved it slowly over Joseph's neck.

"No one moves," Leader added.

The leaves near the boulder rustled, and snow dropped from the bushes, as the wolf crawled closer and closer. We stood frozen in fear at the scene before us. I looked to Pushmataha, and the strength of his gaze told me this was a moment I would never forget.

The wolf must have made the first move, but I will only ever remember Leader stepping over Joseph, raising the point of his sword, and plunging it into the neck of the wolf.

Then the general kicked Joseph out of the way as the wolf rolled and batted the air with its claws, blood spurting in a wide circle, covering Joseph and Leader, the Nahullo soldiers, and our Choctaw family. For one moment, we shared the same grief, the sadness at the end of a life. I hoped someday I could be like Pushmataha and understand what had just taken place.

"I don't know any more than you do," Pushmataha answered.

I looked at him in surprise.

The wise old chief just nodded and smiled.

Leader ordered, "Move the wolf out of the road. I'll send some men back to skin him. Give these people back their blankets, and let's see how far we can walk today."

The general mounted his saddle and was about to ride away, when he tugged the reins and swung his horse around.

"Young man," Leader said, "I expect to see you with your friends from now on. No need to hide."

Joseph stood and nodded, whispering so only his friends could hear him.

"Yakoke. Thank you," he said.

Chapter 12
Dark Memories

WE ONLY WALKED TWO miles that day. The snow fell
thick and the wind was strong, blowing in our faces. We
could not see where we were walking, and many Choctaws
fell, stumbling over stones and the carcasses of frozen an-
imals and birds.

"Should we trust him?" Pushmataha asked as we gathered by the fireside that evening. "He says he will not
harm Joseph, that it's now safe for Joseph to walk with the
others. But should we trust him?"

"I am lucky to be alive," said Joseph. "Somehow I
think the wolf saved my life."

"You may be right," Naomi said. "Until Leader was
reminded of the wolf that almost killed him, he was planning on killing you."

"Can we talk about something besides wolves?" I asked.

Pushmataha smiled and shook his head. "Isaac," he said, "somehow you make us laugh when we want to cry. That's the Choctaw way."

"I had a good teacher."

"Yakoke," he said.

"Oh, you are a good teacher, too, Chief Pushmataha, but I was talking about my dog, Jumper."

Everybody laughed now—Naomi, our mothers and fathers, even Joseph, and Jumper jumped into my lap, licking my face with a cold, wet tongue. Everybody laughed but Pushmataha.

"See how funny you think this is," he said, with that sly Pushmataha look in his eyes.

Whrrrr. Whrrrr.

"Hoke, Chief, that's not funny! You know how scared I am of snakes."

Yes, Stella appeared, sliding her rattlesnake self over my cross-legged lap and slithering up my belly and chest. She didn't stop till her tongue flicked back and forth, like she was about to kiss me. Or kill me.

"Can you make her go away?"

"Can you be more polite?" Pushmataha asked.

"Yes, anything. I'll do anything."

"Will you cook breakfast tomorrow?" Naomi asked.

"Yes. Anything."

"Will you build the fire?" Joseph asked.

Hoke, I could see where this was going. "Yes," I said, folding my arms and making an ugly face.

"Will you take your clothes off and roll around in the snow?" Stella asked. At least I think that's what she said. It's hard to understand somebody when they're hissing and talking at the same time.

"No!" I shouted. "That's asking too much."

"Will you be quiet and let us talk?" Pushmataha asked.

I nodded, and Stella, her old sweet-lady self again, sat beside me.

"Now, can we trust Leader?" Pushmataha asked.

When no one spoke, he cast his eyes around the circle, looking at each of us, reading our thoughts.

"You are correct, Joseph," he finally said. "I should know more about the dangers of trusting the enemy than anyone."

I knew he was remembering General Jackson, kneeling down and tossing the flowers on his coffin, and the words of the soldiers who had killed his friend.

He took a long breath, and the sad look returned to his face.

"We will be grateful for the peace of today," Pushmataha said, "but we must never forget, he can change in a flash. He will always be the Leader who passed out the killing blankets."

Each of us wrapped ourselves in the memories brought on by his mention of the blankets. I saw Old Man and Old Woman sitting in the shallow waters near our home, our Choctaw home. I felt my mother grip my hand as we watched the old couple splash sand on each other's faces, hugging and laughing. I do not want to see this again.

You must, Isaac, this is your memory. What you are seeing happened to the Choctaw people in your town. It was the voice of Pushmataha, whispering through the pines of that long ago morning.

"But why do I keep remembering it?" I asked. "I want it all to go away."

You are remembering the fire and the blankets and the loss of the people you loved for one important reason.

"Why?"

To tell others, Isaac. To honor the people of your town who died, to never forget that they were good people and lived their lives helping others.

I stared ahead and saw the skin on Old Man's face turn red and blister. I saw Old Woman run her fingers across her face and the blood begin to flow.

"Please. I will never forget."

No, Isaac. None of us will forget. We must somehow learn to forgive, but we must never forget.

"Are you here, Son?" my father said.

I closed my eyes, left my memories, and returned to the evening campfire. My family and Naomi's sat close to the fire. Embers popped, and the smell of bubbly, boiling corn stew floated in smoky clouds all around us.

"We miss you, Isaac, but it's so good to know you will never leave us," my mother said, brushing away the tears.

"I miss you, too, Mom. Know I don't feel cold or hungry anymore," I added, hoping to make her happy.

"But you can't enjoy your father's pashofa."

While my mother and father mourned the things I

could no longer do now that I was a ghost, I searched the darkness for any sign of Joseph. I knew he would stay close to our families, but I knew him well enough to know he would never fully trust Leader. I heard a rustling of leaves overhead and realized Joseph wanted to talk.

"I'll be back in a minute," I told my parents, and I joined my friend in the woods.

"There's a conversation you need to hear, Isaac," Panther Joseph said.

Without waiting for me to reply, he dashed away, leaping from one tree to the next, his claws slashing through the icicles. One large branch cracked beneath his weight and fell, but Joseph was gone before it even hit the forest floor.

I was just about to ask myself, *How can we hear a conversation that has already happened?* Suddenly, a dark purple cloud appeared, and Joseph flew from the tree to the cloud and I followed.

Hoke, I thought, *Pushmataha is taking us to the recent past.*

Chapter 13

Leader and the Purple Fire

THROUGH THE PURPLE cloud we flew, joining Push-mataha on a log by the campfire of General Leader and his men, Roundman, Pointy Nose, and the other soldiers.

These were the same men who months ago had dragged Naomi away from camp, as Leader warned her parents, "If she ever tries to escape, or if anyone tries to free her, you will never see that little one again."

He had then pointed at Nita.

But when Nita rolled from her blanket one freezing night and became a ghost, Leader's threat lost its hold on her family. Joseph and I, along with Jumper, helped Naomi escape.

Now here we were, once again, gathered around the fire and eavesdropping again on the dark plans of Leader.

"You have to remember, always, these people are not like us," Leader said. "They are savages. They will kill you if you turn your back on them. That's why we are moving them out of our country, so we can grow our cotton and have our slaves and live in peace."

As we listened, I found myself watching the men sitting around the fire. The same men who had once clung to every word Leader said had now grown tired of his loud, arm-waving rants. I saw men glance at each other when Leader wasn't looking, as if saying *we've heard this before.*

The men now doubted their leader. And how could they not? No Choctaw had tried to kill a single soldier on the Trail and none of my people had burned down a soldier's home or church. Yet, these soldiers had already killed hundreds of Choctaws.

He has no family, I thought.

"You are right, Isaac," Pushmataha said. "This man has no one to care for, no one to protect and love."

"Why does he do these mean things to others?" I asked, and Leader himself answered as he addressed his men.

"I served under General Jackson," Leader said, "and we are once again following his orders. He knows what is best for us all."

At the mention of Jackson, the man I had seen kneel over Pushmataha's grave, I felt a hot breath kick me in the chest and send me floating through the purple cloud, above the snow-covered forest.

"Isaac," Pushmataha whispered. "Do not let him have that much power over you. Come back, we need you."

I felt his strong hand grip me by the shoulders and pull me back to join Joseph, now hovering above the soldiers sitting by the fire.

"We are doing everything he says, aren't we?" asked Pointy Nose.

"So far," Leader replied, "but I don't want any more trouble from that boy. Whatever tricks he does to turn himself into a wildcat, we've got to stop him."

"How can we do that?" Roundman asked.

Leader looked into the fire. He took a sip of coffee and said nothing. Pointy Nose nudged his friend with his elbow, telling him to be quiet. Everyone but Roundman knew what Leader was saying.

Joseph had to be killed.

I felt a warm paw touch my neck, and I knew it was Panther Joseph telling me to listen well; this was why he had brought me here.

"He's a smart one," Leader said. "He might walk with the others when he doesn't see any soldiers, but as soon as we approach, he'll take to the trees. If we're gonna get him, we'll have to sneak up on him."

"Won't be easy, sneaking up on that one. Not easy, I can tell you that," Roundman said.

Pointy Nose rolled his eyes and pretended to watch a butterfly flit and fly over the campfire, but there was no butterfly, only an uneasy silence.

"No," said Leader, "it will not be easy. But I have my own secret weapon I have not used yet."

Everyone around the fire leaned in closer, and I felt a

warm glow settle beside me, the ghost of Pushmataha. The *whirring* of a rattlesnake told me Stella had joined us, and Nita and big sister Naomi appeared as well.

Leader laughed and spit into the fire. "You think I'm going to tell you all what my secret is?"

Everyone waited.

"He's been with us all along, but no one paid him any attention. Not unless they wanted their horse fed or snow shoveled or some other chore done that no one else wanted to do."

"You mean . . ." Roundman started to say, but Pointy Nose elbowed him in the ribs. "Yow! Why did you do that?"

Leader took another sip of coffee and waited for the moment to return to him.

"Yes, I mean Tobert, the only slave among us. He's been sleeping in the woods and walking out of sight so no townspeople could see him, but notice how he's always there when I need him?"

Tobert, as the soldiers called him, had been a worker for one of the families north of our town. Most Choctaws knew him, and we knew other Choctaw families that kept such workers. Some treated them as family members, while others treated them mean and ordered them about, yelling and snapping whips that left backs scarred and spirits broken.

I had seen Tobert during the walk, but he had stayed mostly out of sight. He was a strong, thin man in his early twenties. Although he was treated well by the Choctaw family that had bought him, I knew it was wrong, very wrong—to keep him as if he was their property, to do with as they wished.

Not everything we Choctaws do is right. We all have our faults and we all make mistakes. Once more, the voice of Pushmataha circled us with a blessing and a lesson.

"If you mean that skinny slave who mumbles when he talks and barely has the mind of a tree stump, he can't help us," Roundman said.

Leader took another long sip of coffee and stared at the ground. I knew he was keeping a secret about Tobert from them.

"I have not seen him in a month or more," Pointy Nose said. "And I haven't missed him. I thought you maybe sold him to some townspeople."

"When his owners died in the fire, I had a good long talk with him," Leader said.

His owners! I thought. *No one owns another person.*

Leader continued. "I told him I would make sure he was safe, and when we arrived in Indian country after the walk, I would see that he could go free."

"And he believed you?" Roundman said.

"Of course, he believed me. I was telling him the truth."

I will never know how Pushmataha does it, how he makes time freeze or the world spin or Rattlesnake Stella appear to scare the pants off me at just the right moment, but what happened next came as the biggest surprise yet. Maybe the biggest surprise in a few days. Pushmataha let us see inside the dark and evil mind of this man Leader.

When he said, "I was telling the truth," Leader grew two sharp horns, one on each side of his head. I waited for Roundman to stare at the horns. I waited for Pointy Nose to point his finger at the horns. But nothing happened. The soldiers, all of them, continued looking at the fire and listening to their general. No one raised his eyes or said a word.

They cannot see the horns, I thought, and Pushmataha sent his warm glow in response.

"No, those horns are for only you to see, my Choctaw friends," he whispered.

"Where has he been?" asked Pointy Nose.

"He has kept to the woods ahead of us, well out of sight, for his own safety," Leader said. "We are now in plantation country where slaves are common. If anyone saw him, they would assume he was a runaway slave and either hang him or take him as their own."

Leader peered closely at the circle of faces surrounding the fire. *He is wondering how much to tell them*, I thought.

"That's enough for now," Leader finally said, standing up and tossing the remains of his coffee into the fire. "Let's get some sleep."

Chapter 14
Joseph and the New Danger

JOSEPH, PUSHMATAHA, AND I waited behind as our Choctaw friends returned to the campfire of our families, the campfire of the present. We watched as Pointy Nose threw more branches on the fire and Roundman rolled blankets by the rising flames, hoping for a peaceful night of sleep.

Every snowflake that fell carried a sadness, until a blanket of white blinded us from the hope we clung to, as faithful Choctaws. Our task of rescuing Choctaws from the freezing cold was coming to an end. Now Joseph was the target because Leader wanted him dead.

Joseph climbed down the tree, and I followed him, walking through the forest of time.

"Pushmataha, you were a target, too," said Joseph.

"Yes, Joseph, and my enemies were strong."

"But I have two things that you did not have."

"What two things?"

"One, the knowledge that Leader wants to kill me. You trusted your leader," Joseph said.

"Yes, that is true. And the second?" asked Pushmataha.

"It is why I will stay alive, why I will overcome my enemy," Joseph said.

"Yes?"

"You, Pushmataha, you are my secret weapon. I have you by my side."

As if Pushmataha willed it to happen, the clouds broke and a thin moonbeam fell from the sky to our Choctaw campfire.

I sat close to my family as the fathers snored and the mothers pulled their children close. I know ghosts are not supposed to sleep. Jumper knows that, too. He's been around me long enough to know all about ghosts, especially what they can and cannot do. But that night by the campfire was the closest thing to sleep I have experienced since I became a ghost. Jumper must have spotted me ghost-dozing.

"Time to wake up!" he shouted, jumping onto my lap and slobbering my face with puppy-dog-kisses.

He was right. Everyone else was already awake, piling dry limbs inside the fire circle and boiling snow for pashofa stew, our favorite breakfast.

"Hoke," I said. "Can I say that I'm glad I can't feel your wet tongue?"

"Sure about that?" said Jumper, wagging his tail and leaping around and through me.

"No, you're right, Jumper. I'd give anything to be one of the family again."

"You are part of the family, young man, and don't you ever forget it," my mother said over her shoulder as she gave the pashofa a stir.

I floated into sight, and everybody stopped what he or she was doing to welcome me with a great big Choctaw smile. For those of you who are not Choctaw, imagine the happiest you have ever been in your life, and you'll have some idea of how big a Choctaw smile can be. That lasted for maybe four minutes.

While Naomi served steaming hot pashofa, spooning the thick yellow soup into outstretched bowls, a man entered our camp. He was on foot and had a thick green blanket, the kind worn by the soldiers, wrapped over his shoulders and around his head. I know this may sound like a regular, everyday occurrence. A man walks in from the road and enters the circle where people are sitting around a campfire. After all, it was wintertime, and we were sitting by a snow-covered trail in the woods. Fire is warm and attracts attention, so what made this moment so strange?

Let's see. He was walking, not riding like the soldiers, and he did wear a soldier's blanket. Hoke. What else? Nothing really, nothing you could put your finger on. It was more of a feeling, the way he stepped too close too soon, as if he knocked on the door of our family circle and walked in without being asked.

"Sure smells good," he said, pulling the blanket down so we could see his face. He smiled as he spoke.

"Tobert," I whispered to myself.

Joseph leaned against a tree close by, ready for his breakfast. He jumped to his feet and hid behind the tree trunk. "Is he alone?" he asked.

"Yes, no one else anywhere near."

"I am staying here for now," Joseph said. "If I take even a few steps he'll hear the ice and snow crunch."

"Smart thinking," I said. "If he comes this way I will warn you."

"Tobert," my father said. "I met you once a few years ago. Chim achukma, how are you?"

"Ahm achukma hoke, doing well," Tobert said. "Just cold and hungry."

"Naomi, do we have another bowl?" her mother asked.

Naomi filled another bowl, and my father scooted over on the log, offering Tobert a place to sit.

"We were afraid you died in the fire," Luke said, taking the lead in finding out what had brought Tobert to us.

"I was sleeping in the barn the night the soldiers came," Tobert said. "When I saw the flames and ran from the barn, they knocked me out. I woke up the next morning in the back of a wagon, my feet chained together."

"How did you get away?" Luke asked.

"I did everything they asked of me. I bowed my head and took their beatings. Eventually, they came to trust me. They still do. They told me to walk down the line and see if everybody was hoke. So that's what I am doing."

"I guess they know you won't try to escape in this kind of weather," my father said.

"No place to go," said Tobert.

"We are doing hoke for now," Luke said.

Tobert sat up in surprise at seeing a young man speak for both families.

"We can always use more corn, but we never go hungry," Luke added.

"The same with blankets," Martha said.

"My wife makes sure our little daughter is wrapped tight and warm before she wraps herself," Gabe said.

"Always the children first," Tobert said.

"Even after they die," said Martha, fighting back the tears.

"Oh, I am sorry," Tobert said, seeing for the first time the tiny, still blanket lying at her side. "I didn't know."

"We are hoke here," Luke said, "so after breakfast, you can check on other families if you like."

"I am tired of walking," Tobert said. "If you don't mind I'll just help you folks today."

Everyone nodded and turned their attention to breakfast, but I knew Luke now had his answer. He had wanted to know if Tobert had just happened to stop by our camp for breakfast, or if he had come with a purpose.

"He is looking for me," Joseph whispered. "And he is smart enough not to ask about me, so as not to give himself away."

Chapter 15
Tobert Shows His Hand

"HE DOESN'T HAVE ANY weapons, Joseph," I said as the day's walk began and we moved away from the camp.

"None that you can see," said Joseph. "He was sent to kill me. I have no doubt about that."

"He has to find you first."

"Do you remember how Leader found me?"

"He threatened Naomi," I said, remembering Leader's mean eyes as he urged his horse against her.

We walked in silence for what seemed like hours, both of us thinking of what Leader might do this time.

At noon, the usual resting hour, we stopped in a small grove of trees downslope from the road.

Using broken tree branches, Joseph swept a thick pillow of snow from the ground. He pulled a few strips of dried pork from his pocket. "Want one?" he asked, holding a pork strip under my nose.

"You know I'd fight you for it if I was still alive," I said, laughing.

"Hoke," he replied, "then you could blame me for your final day, instead of that wolf."

I knew why he was teasing me. Joseph was Choctaw, and whether panther or human, he felt guilty eating while I could not. "Hey," I said, "you gotta live with hunger and cold and cuts and bruises, so stop worrying about me."

The warm silence that followed was short-lived.

"I thought I'd find you here," Tobert said, sliding down the hill and landing next to Joseph. "Who were you talking to?"

"Nobody. Just myself."

"Well, it's great to see you, Joseph. People are still talking about you, up and down the line, how you saved Leader, and then he pardoned you. Why aren't you walking with everybody else?"

"I don't like all the noise that people bring."

"Oh. Sorry. I'm just excited to see you. For a long time, I thought you were dead."

And you have come to finish the job, I thought.

"Nope. Sorry to disappoint you," Joseph said.

Tobert looked over his shoulder and leaned closer to Joseph, lowering his voice to a whisper. "That's what I wanted to talk to you about, away from the others."

Joseph moved away from him. We were only fifty feet from the road but hidden by mounds of snow. Tobert could muffle Joseph's cries and stab him, and no one would ever know. It might be spring before his body was found.

I floated into sight, standing over them. "You know you are never alone when you're with Choctaws," I said.

"Hoke, achukma," Tobert said, jumping back in surprise. "Where did you come from? You're not alive, are you?"

"Yes, I am alive," I said. "Alive enough to still be with my friends and family."

"Sorry, I didn't mean anything by it," Tobert said. "Of course, you're alive."

Seeing how nervous Tobert was, Joseph asked the obvious question. "Why are you here?"

"That is what I want to talk to you about," Tobert said. "Your life is in danger, surely you know that. Leader can be trusted 'only so far as you can throw him,' as my grandmother used to say."

"And who was your grandmother?" Joseph asked.

"Why are you asking me that?"

"Because I want to know," said Joseph. "And tell us why you are here."

"You may not believe me, but I am here to honor my grandmother." Before continuing, Tobert paused, took a deep breath, and looked at both of us for a long time.

"My pokoni, my grandmother, was Choctaw," he said in a whisper of respect, "and we were very close. My grandfather, my amafo, was a slave who escaped from the fields. I was raised speaking Choctaw, in a Choctaw town. My Choctaw name is Luksi Haksinchi."

"A turtle filled with surprises," said Joseph.

"Yes," Tobert said, "and I often surprise myself."

"Halito, Luksi," Joseph said. He reached in his pocket and handed Tobert a strip of dried pork.

"Now, why are you here?"

"I have been sent to kill you," Tobert said, reaching into his own pocket. I had seen Joseph become the panther many times, but never as quickly as he did at those words. Joseph lifted his arms to his chest and his hands to his face to protect himself from the knife we knew Tobert surely carried, but in place of Joseph's fingers were now ten sharp claws.

Panther Joseph swatted Tobert's neck and threw his full weight upon him. Tobert fell backwards, and the knife flew from his hand and into the bushes.

"Wait! No!" Tobert shouted, rolling away and scrambling to retrieve his knife.

I expected Panther Joseph would sink his teeth into Tobert's neck as he had the wolf that killed me. But as Tobert crawled to the bushes, he instead climbed a tree and leapt to safety, leaving our enemy lying in the snow and grateful to be alive.

I let Tobert see me follow Panther Joseph through the trees, but not for long. I needed to see what Tobert would do when he thought he was alone. I closed my eyes and lifted myself high above the forest, then soft as a breeze I returned to Tobert.

As I expected, he was still groping around in the bushes, breaking branches and icicles, looking for his knife. For half an hour, he pawed through the snow and brambles but found nothing.

"Maybe that's a good thing," I said, coming into sight.

Tobert sat cross-legged in the snow and bowed his head, as if to say, "Why does this not surprise me, your being here?"

"And why is any of what has happened a good thing?" he asked.

"Joseph could have killed you," I said. "Now that you have lost your knife, maybe you will go back to Leader and tell him you couldn't finish the job you were sent to do."

"I never intended to do Leader's work."

"You went for your knife. We both saw you. So why lie?" I asked, but I never received a reply.

"Tobert, is that you?" a voice shouted from the road.

"Yes, sir, I'm coming," Tobert yelled, but in a different voice—a servant's voice. Digging his boots into the snow, one careful step at a time, he made his way up the icy slope and stood before the soldier astride his horse.

"What are you doing way off in the woods?" the soldier asked.

Tobert glanced over his shoulder before replying, and I knew he was thinking about me, knowing I would hear every word he said.

"I was down the hill with that panther boy, sir. I aimed to kill him, but before I could, he climbed up that tree and was gone to who knows where."

"And just what do you plan on doing now?"

"Well, sir, I'm not giving up. No, that boy has to die, just like Leader says. I guess I'll have to sneak up on him. He's not that hard to find. I know where he hangs out, close to the girl Naomi."

"Leader won't like it when I tell him you let the boy get away. But if you think you know where he is, move along down the road and find him."

"Yes, sir," said Tobert. "But do tell Leader I've got killing on my mind, and I won't rest till it's done."

"You tell him!" said the soldier. "By this time tomorrow, you better be able to tell him how you killed that panther boy."

He watched as Tobert walked in the direction of my family's camp. When Tobert rounded a curve in the road, the soldier yanked the reins of his horse and rode away.

Chapter 16

Tobert's Lost Knife

I LIFTED MYSELF ABOVE the road and followed Tobert. He soon left the road and returned to the woods. I expected him to find our family and hide out in the nearby forest, waiting for Joseph, just like he had told the soldier he would do.

But as soon as the soldier turned away, Tobert dashed back to the site of our conversation. Once more he rolled to the ground, searching under every bush and fallen tree limb, shoveling snow with his hands and looking for his knife.

He searched till nightfall, resting only once to catch his breath and shake the snow from his hair. Small fires soon appeared, like twinkling fireflies of hope, and Tobert climbed once more to the road. He paused and looked in both directions, to Leader's camp and south to my family's evening fire.

He knows better than to return to Leader with Joseph still alive, I thought. I flew as quick as I could and joined my family. Smoke rose and twisted in the cold breeze, and I wished more than ever that I could taste the corn soup bubbling over the fire.

"You can't have everything," a sweet voice said from below.

I smiled and settled beside Jumper. "How did the day go for you?" I asked.

"Better than for you," Jumper said. "I've never seen Joseph so scared, not even when Leader held his sword over him."

"He is still afraid for Naomi," I said. "He knows she is their bait to bring him out. Leader sent Tobert to kill him. Do you remember him?"

"Yes, I do. So that explains why Joseph is staying hidden," Jumper said.

"Do you know where he is?"

"Why are asking me? All you have to do is step to the woods, and he'll find you," Jumper said.

I smiled and patted my sweet pup on the shoulders. "Hoke," I said, "see you next summer."

"If you're lucky," Jumper replied.

I wished I could spend time with my family, to let them know I was still nearby and watching over them, but Joseph was in danger and needed my help. I searched the woods and hills near the campsite. No Joseph.

He's being careful, I thought. *Smart man.*

I didn't want Tobert to find him before I did.

Where is the last place Tobert would look for Joseph? As soon as I asked myself the question, I knew the answer. The bonepickers! That's where he's hiding. I took one more look at the two families around the campfire, and sure enough, Naomi was missing. Joseph wouldn't leave without her, and that's the safest place to go. No one walks with the bonepickers.

I rose above the camp and flew toward the bonepickers' wagon. I soon spotted their evening fire, with four thin ladies huddled close, their blankets hiding any trace of skin or hair. Just as I was about to land, I spotted movement in the woods.

Hoke, there's Joseph, I thought, *and I bet Naomi's with him, both of them safe and alive.*

I almost said his name aloud, and I'm so glad I didn't, because as I flew closer I saw that I was wrong, very wrong. Somebody was hiding in the woods near the bonepickers' wagon, but it wasn't Joseph or Naomi. It was Tobert crouching in the woods, just out of sight of the flickering flames.

He's smarter than I thought.

As I hovered over him, Tobert moved without a sound, circling the camp. *He must be looking for Joseph.* He soon turned away from the camp and headed to the woods. Pushing aside ice-covered branches, he settled in a clump of frozen bushes.

Good hiding place for the night, I thought.

Only Tobert was not there to hide.

"Do you think he will find us here?"

I recognized the voice as Naomi's. Tobert had already found them and was hiding not ten steps away.

"Not for a few days, anyway," Joseph said.

I had to do something. In that moment, I would have given anything to be alive again. But I didn't want to be a kid like me. No, I wanted to be a strong young man like my brother Luke, strong enough to swoop down and save my friends.

"Anything?" Of course. Pushmataha is everywhere.

"Yes, Pushmataha," I said. "Please, can't we do something? I know we can't change the past, but this is happening now. I do not want to watch my best friend die."

"That's not what you are seeing, Isaac. Tobert doesn't have his knife, remember?"

"I'm not waiting. I've got to warn them," I said.

"Isaac, trust me. Now is not the time for your warnings. If you cause trouble you might be the cause of Joseph's death."

I did trust Pushmataha, but I also trusted my eyes. I watched as Tobert picked up a stone as big as a full-grown turtle and crawled behind Joseph.

Chapter 17

To Live or Die

"IF HE LIFTS THAT STONE, I'm going in," I said.

"So am I," said Pushmataha.

We watched as Tobert held the stone at his side. He sat as quiet as the coming dawn, now only a few feet behind Naomi and Joseph. He finally spoke. "Joseph."

Naomi jumped in terror, and Joseph became the panther, twirling around and waving his claws at Tobert.

"Please," Tobert said. "I am risking my life by being here. Look, I have a stone." He lifted his right arm and showed them the heavy stone. "I could have struck you with it, but I did not."

Panther Joseph throated a low and threatening growl as he settled between Tobert and Naomi. He was still on his haunches, alert and ready to attack.

"I never wanted to hurt you, Joseph. I am Chatah, like you. Leader is not my leader."

What happened next was as unbelievable as anything yet. The voice of Joseph came from the mouth of the panther: "You tried to kill me yesterday," the panther said. "I saw you go for your knife, and you said you were going to kill me."

Panther Joseph turned to Naomi—just long enough for Tobert to relax and lower the stone—then the panther flung himself on top of Tobert, digging his claws deep into his enemy's throat.

"You came here to kill me, liar!" the panther said. "If I hadn't heard you, you would have bashed my head in with the stone. Were you going to kill Naomi, too, and so close to her grieving mother?"

Tobert closed his eyes and shook with fear. "Chahta sia hoke," he whispered. "I am proud to be Choctaw. I suffer as you suffer and I have come to help you."

The panther dug his claws in deeper and red blood drops rose from the wounds. Tobert bowed his head and waited, preparing for his death if that was to be the night's fate.

I held my breath and watched as the panther's black hair sunk into the face of Joseph, but the claws remained. *He does not know what to do*, I realized.

Joseph looked at Naomi, who had already stepped forward, but she shook her head back and forth, and rivers of tears streamed down her cheeks. Naomi did not know whether to trust the intruder Tobert and risk their lives, or nod and watch yet another killing take place on her behalf.

I looked to Pushmataha, and for a brief moment, time froze. The conversation between Tobert and Joseph ceased as we floated above in silence.

"Are you hiding his knife so he can't hurt Joseph?" I asked him.

"No," Chief Pushmataha said. "I hope he finds his knife. I want you all to see it."

"Why? He tried to kill Joseph."

"He was reaching in his pocket for his knife, Isaac, to show it to Joseph."

"He said he was going to kill him."

"No, he said Leader sent him to kill Joseph."

"Isn't that the same thing?" I asked.

Once again, Pushmataha let the silence deliver his lesson. He waited patiently for me to see his meaning.

"He was not there to follow Leader's orders, was he?" I asked. "He is on our side."

"Yes, Isaac, Tobert is one of us, mistreated by Leader and doing his best to stay alive. Now, listen to him," he said, gesturing to the conversation below.

"I did reach for my knife, but not to kill you," Tobert said. "I wanted to show you my Choctaw father's knife. He gave it to me before he died."

"Why did you want me to see it?" Joseph asked. With every word from his mouth, the hair of the panther receded, and my young friend revealed himself.

"Because the knife is old and the blade broke off years ago," Tobert said. "I could not harm a funi with that knife. It wouldn't hurt a squirrel."

"So where is the knife now?" Joseph asked.

"I wish I knew," Tobert said. "It belonged to my father, and I will not leave these woods without it. I spent most of the day yesterday looking for it."

I was staring at the bloody claw marks on his throat, knowing the paw of Panther Joseph held the key to life or death for Tobert. The claws pulled in and fingers of a hand replaced them. Naomi saw the change, too, and took a deep breath, knowing that the threat of death had left us for the moment.

Maybe it was the thought of the many deaths we had seen since the soldiers came to our community, maybe it was the sight of his own home consumed in flames and his grandparents trapped inside, maybe it was just the power of the moment, but whatever picture appeared in Joseph's mind, it was full of grief.

Joseph flung himself once more on Tobert's chest, sinking his claws into his scalp until blood rained from Tobert's head. "You crept behind us with a stone! How can I trust you?" screamed Panther Joseph.

"If he kills Tobert, he will bring death to my family— to us all," I whispered, reaching for Pushmataha. "Please do something."

"Sometimes inaction is the strongest fist," he said, looking deep into my ghost eyes.

"Joseph," said Naomi, "he's telling the truth. Look at him."

"No," said Tobert, "don't look at me. I have done so much bad in my life with Leader and his men. I am ashamed and maybe I deserve to die. But I do not want to see you hurt, either of you."

The panther vanished in a blink of an eye. Joseph was with us again. "Let me help you up," he told Tobert.

Pushmataha held his right fist in front of my face and slowly lifted one finger at a time, as if he were counting. Achufa, tuklo, tuchina, ushtah. One, two, three, four fingers, and at the count of four, he pointed at Joseph, who spoke.

"I do believe you," Joseph said, "and I want to help you find your knife."

If ever we doubted that Tobert was Choctaw, his next words proved it for me. "I know who can help us," Tobert said. "Our people who have gone before, the Choctaw ghosts that walk with us."

"I think I heard my name," said Pushmataha, smiling.

And from the cloud of our ghostly world, he floated into sight. He was joined by Old Man and Old Woman, and then a thousand others appeared—many from our own town. Joseph smiled and cried at the sight of his grandparents.

The crowd of Choctaw ghosts hummed our sacred song, "Shilombish Holitopama," and swayed back and forth in a wave of timeless family. Nita jumped on my back and wrapped her arms around my neck.

"Tobert," a voice called from the center of the throng. "I have something you've been seeking."

From the center of our gathering stepped a man who looked like Tobert, only older.

By his side stood his mother, judging by the smile on her face. Tobert stepped forward, and his father opened his palm to reveal the knife.

"I thought about fixing the blade," he said. "But your mother said 'maybe that's not a good idea just now,' and I think she was right."

"Yakoke, Mother," said Tobert, shaking his head and laughing. "I think you saved my life. This panther here," he said, wrapping his arm around Joseph and pulling him to his side, "he maybe might have ripped my throat out had the blade been fixed."

"Yes," Joseph said, laughing as he spoke, "I maybe would have flung his guts to the treetops."

"Do you hear what you are saying?" Naomi whispered, her eyes bulging and her palms lifted to the sky. "How can you two laugh about such things?"

"We are Choctaws," Pushmataha said, stepping forward and laughing so hard he could barely speak. "If we can't laugh, how can we live?"

With that, a thousand ghosts bellowed out a Choctaw belly laugh that echoed through the woods. Birds flew to join us. I think I even heard the Bishkinik, our Choctaw happy bird, and Gabe and Martha and my family, Mom and Dad and Luke—all of them and many more from nearby camps—as they joined us in the chilly morning warmed by our laughter.

When the laughter settled, Tobert wrapped his arms around his ghost parents and whispered, "Yakoke. I love you both so much. Have you been with me all this time?"

"Always," said his mother. "We are proud of you, my son. Luksi Haksinchi, my Choctaw son."

Led by the older women from our town—the women who had jumped from the pier to say good-bye to our home—we raised our voices and sang our song of praise.

> *Shilombish Holitopama*
> *Ishminti pullacha*
> *Hatak ilbasha pi yaha*
> *Isminti Ishpi yukpa lashki*

Chapter 18
Leader's Anger, Tobert's Lie

"LET'S GO! TIME TO WALK!" shouted the soldier, riding up and down the line.

Breakfast was over and Choctaw families were already clearing camp. Many stood by the ice-covered road, wrapped tight in their blankets and ready for the day's journey.

I wonder what today will bring, I thought.

"Whatever happens, Isaac, Tobert will have to play it smart to be alive at sunset."

I tilted my head in a question and glanced over my shoulder at my chief. Pushmataha rubbed my hair and smiled, acknowledging my efforts to "not talk so much."

"Leader," he said, "will be very angry when he does not receive the news he wants—proof that Joseph is dead."

We rose a hundred feet above the camp and watched my family begin the long, cold walk of the day.

"I wish I could help them," I said.

"You help them more than you will ever know, just by staying close and comforting them in their grief over your loss," Pushmataha said.

"What can Tobert do?" I asked.

"His fate is in his own hands now. We can be there to help him, but I am afraid we cannot save him from his fate. He has defied Leader."

Naomi joined her family as they climbed to the road and left their tracks in the snow of this life. I watched the tracks differently now, the winding twisting trail of footprints that lead all of life to the same destination.

"As long as you understand these tracks are not the end of life, good Isaac," Pushmataha said, reading once again my thoughts.

"Yakoke, Pushmataha," I said. "You are like my new father, my ghost father. Is that hoke?"

"I am very proud to be your ghost father."

We floated together in silence as the sky fired brilliant colored arrows from the bow of dawn, shafts of pink and orange with tips of feather red, surrounded by lighter shades of blue, till the first burst of light lifted over the mountains and we lingered in the sky, two ghosts in awe of the beauty of the day.

"The gifts of the day are different for every one of us," Pushmataha said, pointing to the forest.

Two young men came into sight, Tobert and Joseph.

Once deadly enemies—or so it had seemed—they now walked together in the forest, close to my family but unseen by the soldiers on horseback.

"Let us see what Leader has to say about the evening," Pushmataha said, and next we appeared above the soldier's wagon.

Leader sat next to Roundman, who held the reins and drove the horses. "Did you even feed these horses?" Leader asked, elbowing Roundman in the ribs.

"Yes, sir, General, every morning and today, too," said a very nervous Roundman.

"Make them go faster!" Leader yelled. "I'll be dead by the time we get to Memphis."

Roundman covered his face and fake-coughed, hiding his thoughts from Leader. But the look on his face was clear—the sooner the better.

Pushmataha smiled and shook his head. "You better be glad I'm not that kind of a father," he said.

"Not a problem," I replied. "My ribs wouldn't feel it anyway." *Yeah*, I thought. *I got the last word on Pushmataha!*

"Do I need to call Rattlesnake Stella?"

"No, please, Chief Pushmataha, sir, I'll be a good little boy."

We both had to laugh at that declaration. While we jostled and played father-son games, a soldier approached Leader's wagon, and Roundman pulled the horses to a halt. We floated closer and listened.

"General, I rode by Naomi's family and saw no sign of either Tobert or the panther boy."

"Did you stay out of sight?" Leader asked.

"Yes, sir, and I left my horse by the roadside and searched the nearby woods. Again, not a sign of either. I can order more men to keep a lookout, and if you like, we can surround the families with well-armed soldiers."

"Tobert is too smart for that," Leader said. "No, we need to be as quiet as possible. Who is the smallest and quickest among us?"

In the brief pause of thought, I saw Roundman turn his face away and tighten his lips.

"He knows the answer to that one," I whispered.

"Yes," nodded Pushmataha. "His friend Pointy Nose."

"He's riding behind you, General," the soldier said, nodding in the direction of Pointy Nose. "He's fast enough to stay up with Tobert, and if we find Tobert we should also find the panther boy."

"I don't know if anyone is fast enough to run with Tobert," Leader said, "but he's our best chance. Alright, bring him to me."

"You wanted to see me, Leader?" said Pointy Nose, riding his horse alongside the wagon and trying to hide his enthusiasm.

"Tobert has disappeared, along with the panther boy."

"Are we sure Tobert is still alive?" Pointy Nose asked. "I know I wouldn't want to find that black demon in the woods."

"That's too bad, Sergeant, because that is exactly what I am ordering you to do. Find the black demon and Tobert, too. You are to tie your horse to the wagon and make your way deep into the forest. I recommend taking a backpack of dried food and supplies, but travel light."

"Yes, sir."

"The panther boy must not see you or suspect you are seeking him, is that understood?"

"Yes, sir, I understand."

"I do not want Tobert to see you either. Stay in the woods, make no fires, and talk to no one, not even a fellow soldier. Is that understood?"

"Yes, sir," Pointy Nose said, taking a deep breath and keeping his eyes locked on Leader's.

"Are you strong enough to do this?"

"Yes, General, I am. What should I do when I find them?"

"Kill them both," Leader said, without hesitation. "I am ordering you to kill them both."

Pointy Nose opened his mouth to speak, but the words hung on his lips, and he looked to the ground.

"You have something to say?" Leader asked.

"No, sir. I will follow your orders without question."

"Pushmataha, he wants to know why he should kill Tobert."

"Yes, Isaac. But you know, don't you?"

"I think I do. When people are no longer useful to him, Leader doesn't care if they live or die. And if he kills Joseph, Tobert is more dangerous to him alive."

"I could not have said it better myself, Son."

We watched from high overhead as Pointy Nose readied himself for the most dangerous journey of his life. He climbed into the back of the wagon and loaded a small backpack with dried strips of pork. He found a knife with a long blade and a small pistol with several rounds of ammunition. In less than ten minutes, he tied his horse to the rear of the wagon and appeared at Leader's side.

"I am ready to go, sir," he said.

"Good luck to you, Sergeant. I hope to see you in two days, if not sooner, with reports of the deaths of our enemies."

"Yes, sir," Pointy Nose replied, with a sharp salute and a click of his boot heels.

Chapter 19

Nita to the Rescue

"I DON'T LIKE where this is going," I said.

Pushmataha only tightened his lips and nodded. I followed him as we rose far above the snow-covered forest.

"Shouldn't we warn Joseph?"

"Isaac, Joseph knows all he needs to know. He knows he will never be safe on the trail with his family, as long as Leader is alive."

"I want to warn Naomi," I said. "She needs to know to be careful of Pointy Nose."

"Don't you think she already knows that, Isaac? He was so mean to her when she lived with the soldiers, she'll never forget that."

"I have a plan."

"You have a plan you don't want to share with me?"

Pushmataha asked, wrinkling his brow and doing his best to hide his smile.

"There comes a time when a son must strike out on his own," I said, puffing out my chest.

"I'm with Isaac," Jumper said, appearing by my side with his tail wagging, as usual.

"Looks like you two have ganged up on me," said Pushmataha. "Two against one! I don't have a chance. Of course, there was that Battle of New Orleans, when our Choctaw battalion was badly outnumbered. If memory serves me correctly, we not only won but also demolished the enemy."

"Hoke, hoke," I said. "Chief Pushmataha, with all due respect, Jumper and I are not your enemies."

Jumper growled a low threatening growl, lowered himself as if about to pounce on Pushmataha, and bared his shiny little teeth.

"Jumper, stop it," I said. "That's not funny."

However, Pushmataha thought it was. He covered his mouth and tried not to laugh.

"Please, I just want to try one little plan. Just one. And if you don't like it, you can stop it before it starts."

"I give you my full blessing."

"Yakoke," I said, flying away as fast as I could, with Jumper close behind, before the general had time to change his mind.

"What did you get us into?" Jumper asked.

"Don't worry, you'll like the plan. Nita is involved."

"Yes!" Jumper barked.

I knew Pushmataha was nearby, staying respectfully out of sight. I also knew what he would do if he didn't like my plan.

He'll send Rattlesnake Stella after us, I thought. I was glad Jumper couldn't read my thoughts. He was terrified of Rattlesnake Stella.

We soon flew over our families, huddled together and struggling to stay warm. They walked against a heavy storm, the wind stinging any piece of skin not covered by a blanket. My mother held tight to my father's waist. The two men—or maybe I should say the three men, Gabe, my dad, and Luke—walked in the lead to take the full force of the storm. Naomi often joined the men, I noticed.

"She has overcome much more than a snowstorm," I whispered.

"I am proud she is my sister," a tiny girl's voice whispered back at me.

"Nita," I said, "I was hoping to find you here."

Sweet little Nita came into sight before me, spinning like a puppy chasing his tale. "It's me!" she squealed.

"Hoke, Nita, stop—you're making me dizzy."

"Sorry!" She floated beside me, kissing my ear.

"Maybe this wasn't such a good plan after all," Jumper said.

"What plan?" Nita asked.

I could almost hear the ghost of Pushmataha. *Yes, Isaac, what exactly is this magic plan of yours?*

"Nita, I know how much you love your sister, and you know that Joseph saved her life, right?"

"Yes, so I love Joseph, too."

"Achukma," I said. "I'm here to bring you bad news and good news both. Bad news first. Leader, the meanest man we know, has sent Sergeant Pointy Nose to kill Joseph."

"Noooo!" cried Nita.

"Wait," I said, "that's just the bad news. Here's the good news. You have been chosen to be the messenger. The soldiers can't see you, but when you want them to, Joseph and Naomi can. So you can follow Pointy Nose and warn them if he gets close. What do you think about that?"

"I like it, Isaac. Finally somebody sees I'm a strong Choctaw, too."

"Chatah sia hoke," I said. "Here's something else you should know. Joseph is not alone. A man who used to be a slave, Tobert, is with him. Leader wants them both dead."

"I remember Tobert," Nita said. "He passed through town a few times, driving a wagon."

"Yes, that's the same Tobert. He is now a good friend, and he even told us that his mother is Choctaw."

"I will look out for him, too."

"Achukma, Nita. That's what I was hoping. Now, here's what I want you to do. First, when no one else is listening, tell Naomi everything I just told you, about Pointy Nose and Joseph and Tobert."

"My mother will start crying again when she knows Joseph might become a ghost."

"That's why we need to keep our plan a secret for now," I said.

"Hoke, I understand. I can only tell Naomi."

"Yes. And come find me after you do that, hoke? I'll be with Pushmataha, looking for Pointy Nose. He won't be riding his horse like before. He's sneaking through the woods."

"This will be like being in two places at once."

"Can you do that?"

"Yes," Nita said, with a sweet determined look on her face, "any good ghost can be in two places at once."

"Achukma, Nita. Now, I must be going. Chipisa latchiki," I called out over my shoulder. "See you soon."

As I rose above the forest, a thin moonbeam knifed through the clouds and shone down upon me.

What is happening? I thought, and in reply, I heard the deep, soft laughter of Chief Pushmataha. *He is letting me know he likes my plan, and in a very Choctaw way. Even in the toughest of times, we find reasons to be happy.*

The laughter was short-lived. Pointy Nose knew the first place to look for Choctaws. As Pushmataha said, we are people of the water.

Joseph and Tobert were camped two miles from the trail on the bank of a swift flowing river. The surface was covered with a thin sheet of ice, but with the first day of full sunlight, I knew the ice would soon be washed downstream.

With several small hills and the thick forest separating them from the soldiers, Joseph and Tobert had built a small fire, covered it with pine branches and blankets, and were now cooking a late-night meal.

Ushtah funis, four small squirrels, rolled and popped in the grease of a clay frying pan. Joseph and Tobert huddled close to the flames for warmth. Even as cautious as he was, Joseph would never have suspected that Pointy Nose, or any other soldier, could find them in such a remote spot.

Pointy Nose leaned against the thick trunk of an old oak tree, a stone's throw from their camp and out of sight with his back to the fire. He held his pistol to his chest, waiting for the right moment to step into the camp and shoot them both.

I wanted to drop from the sky and warn them, to urge them to kick the fire out and dive for the bushes. But I did not.

Instead, I asked myself, *What would Pushmataha do?*

I knew the answer. He would ignore his first impulse and consider the smartest action, not the quickest. *Sometimes speed is important, I could almost hear him say, but sometimes speed of thought is the best path to take.*

So I waited, looking again at the three men who huddled in the cold before me. Pointy Nose is not sure what to do either, I realized. If he were, Tobert and Joseph would already be on the ground, bleeding from their wounds.

I could see my two friends easily, but I'm a ghost and I see things regular people cannot. Pointy Nose saw only the shadows of two men through a thick wall of pine branches and blankets.

He will wait till they are eating, I thought. I've had enough fried squirrel to know you can't take your eyes off the tiny, bony pieces of meat or you will burn your hands.

Jumper licked my neck the first time I burned myself on fried squirrel and threw the meat in the air. He caught the squirrel before it hit the ground and had his best supper ever.

Hoke, I could be very quiet and careful and warn them that Pointy Nose is nearby. But when he saw them doing anything unusual, he would step into the camp and start firing his gun. At least one of them would be hit, and he would shoot at Joseph first. That's what Leader would want.

Pushmataha has to be close, I thought. *If you tell me what to do, I will do it*, I thought-told him.

"You're doing fine, Isaac," he whispered.

I should have known he would bring his secret weapon. I heard something crawling across the frozen leaves at the foot of the tree near Pointy Nose. The leaves cracked and rattled, and soon the sound of rattles grew louder.

Whirrrr. Whirrrr.

Achukma! Rattlesnake Stella, my true best friend in the whole world, at least when I needed her. Hoke, I knew this was a life-and-death situation, but if Stella was here so was Pushmataha, and I couldn't help myself.

This is going to be fun! I thought.

Stella did not disappoint. She slithered over the boots of Pointy Nose, and when he looked down, his eyes filled with not fear but terror—absolute terror. He kicked his right leg into the air and sent her flying. Stella landed on a boulder slippery with ice and tried to wiggle her way to the top.

It must be tough not having any hands, I thought, watching as Stella waved her tail and fangs, yet couldn't stop herself from sliding into a bush of thorny needles. The needles stuck into her skin like she was a pincushion, and she whipped herself into a rope and spun away, more angry than I had ever seen her. I know steam isn't supposed to rise from the nostrils of a rattlesnake, but I'm a witness that it can happen. Stella flashed her angry eyes and hissed so loudly her fangs waved like palm trees in a Gulf Coast hurricane.

I wouldn't want to be Pointy Nose, I thought.

Neither did Pointy Nose, but he didn't get to choose. The thick tree trunk blocked the light of the fire, so Pointy Nose was in the dark. Stella crept up beside him and once she realized he couldn't see her, she taunted him to the point of madness. She hid beneath a flat stone, stuck out her tail, and rattled a soft song, then yanked her tail to safety as he took off his boot and slapped the ground.

Dumb move. Very dumb.

Pulling in her poisonous fangs, Stella opened wide her enormous mouth and bit him on his left big toe.

"Yowwwww!" he hollered—loud enough to wake the dead, as Nahullos sometimes say, but since I am a ghost and clearly understand that the dead never sleep, this no longer makes any sense to me.

Nevertheless, his screams did call Tobert and Joseph to action. They flung snow on the fire and took to the shadows. What happened next was even more surprising.

In a flash, Rattlesnake Stella became Stella the Choctaw elder, standing over the cowering figure of Pointy Nose.

He was curled up on the ground, hiding his face with his hands and muttering, "Please don't hurt me, please don't hurt me . . ." over and over.

"You want me not to hurt you when you are here to kill two Choctaws?" Stella said.

"Only one," he said. "I was sent to kill the Choctaw panther boy and the slave."

"That makes two Choctaws," Joseph said.

He and Tobert, along with Stella, now stood over Pointy Nose, the soldier sent to kill them.

"What do you mean?" Pointy Nose asked, wiping his nose with his sleeve and staring at the ground.

"He means I might have been a field worker, what you rudely call a *slave*," Tobert said, "but I am also Choctaw. My father helped my mother escape and married her. I was born a member of the Choctaw Nation, and I will die a Choctaw."

"But not today," Joseph said. "He will not die today."

As he spoke, a beam of moonlight parted the clouds, and Pushmataha appeared.

"No, Joseph," Pushmataha said, in his quiet and powerful voice. "No Choctaws will die today, not at the hands of this soldier."

"If you let me go, I will never hurt any of you again," Pointy Nose said, still unable to lift his eyes.

"You would like to go?"

"Yes, if you will let me."

"First, Sergeant, you have a choice to make," said Pushmataha. "If you choose to live, you may ride your horse tonight, far away from us."

"Yes," Pointy Nose said, "thank you. I will go and never hurt any Choctaws. Never. Where is my horse?"

"Your horse is nearby, on the other side of the river." Pointy Nose lifted his chin and peered across the icy waters.

"Your gun and knife have been replaced with dried pork, enough for several days," Pushmataha continued. "You will also find a blanket on your saddle."

"Can I go now?"

"As soon as you remove your uniform," Pushmataha said. "You have betrayed your promise to us, to lead us safely to our new home."

"I don't understand."

"You have a choice, as I said. You may return to Leader and tell him what happened, everything—about the rattlesnake, about seeing Choctaw ghosts, about being discovered."

"Leader will kill me."

"Then I recommend the other option."

"What is that?"

"You will leave your uniform here, along with your weapons. Joseph is about your size. You can wear his clothes."

Pointy Nose stared at Pushmataha as if he had just declared the end of the world. He shook his head, faster and faster, and finally blurted out, "No! I cannot wear that boy's clothes. If the soldiers see me, they will kill me. I won't do it."

"Sergeant, you will no longer be a soldier. You can wade across the river, climb on your horse, and ride away.

You can make a new home for yourself, somewhere in these mountains."

Pointy Nose rocked back and forth, shivering and blubbering like a scared child. Without a word, he pulled off his other boot, removed his clothes, and tossed them to the ground.

"Joseph!" Pushmataha said, gesturing to the tree.

Joseph stepped behind the tree and removed his clothes. He tossed them to Pointy Nose, who angrily dressed. With one final deep breath, as if he were saying good-bye to the life he knew, Pointy Nose dashed to the river. He held his pointed nose and dipped beneath the waters.

We stood and watched as he appeared on the opposite shore. He grabbed the blanket, dried himself off as best he could, and mounted his horse. Rather than cross the shore, where his past awaited, Pointy Nose rode up the mountainside and into the darkness.

"That is the last time we will ever see him," I said.

"You know better than that," Pushmataha replied.

Chapter 20

Nita on the Prowl

"I'M SORRY," said Nita, with her bottom lip poking out and a sad look on her face.

"Why are you sorry?" I asked.

"I was too scared to do anything. I didn't help."

"Nita, you did what we all needed you to do. You were quiet and you waited," said Pushmataha. "Look, Joseph and Tobert are alive and Pointy Nose is gone."

"Hoke!" Nita squealed. "Then I am happy!"

"But if you still want to help," I said, "you can follow Pointy Nose and report back to us."

"But never let anyone see you," added Pushmataha. "Can you do that?"

"Yes, sir," said Nita.

And with a sharp salute worthy of a military man, she

flew across the river in pursuit of the unfortunate Pointy Nose.

In the silence that followed, Pushmataha gestured with his palms for us all to have a seat. He hung his head in prayer and we followed him, closing our eyes while he whispered words of yakoke, words of thanks.

"Amen," he said when he finished, then looked to Joseph. "Let's not take any chances with the uniform. Roll it up like a log and place it on the campfire."

"What am I supposed to wear?" asked Joseph.

"Isaac, can you find Choctaw clothes for Joseph to wear?" Pushmataha asked.

"If he doesn't mind wearing them, I saw extra clothes in a wagon behind us," I said.

"I am afraid to ask which wagon," said Joseph.

"Hoke," I said, "so what if the clothes belong to those in the care of the bonepickers? They're good clean Choctaw clothes. I saw them wash the clothes in the river."

"I think we have a plan," Pushmataha said.

"Yes," said Tobert. "I am glad we have a plan."

All eyes went to our newest Choctaw friend.

"That's hoke," he said. "I'm used to being left out."

Pushmataha leaned back and tossed his laughter to the sky, and we all had to smile, even Tobert.

"You will never again be left out, Tobert, not among us!"

He wrapped his arms around Tobert's shoulders and we Choctaws knew what to do next.

We sang the "Friendship" song.

Yada hadayama
Yada hadayamah
Yada hadayamah
Yadah hayama.

Four times we sang the song, nodding and encouraging Tobert to learn the simple words so he could join in with us. When he did, for the last verse, we made a circle by touching shoulders with those next to us and sang so sweet and soft it was a holy moment.

Yada hadayama
Yada hadayamah
Yada hadayamah
Yadah hayama.

"Now that you are one of us," Pushmataha said, "you're probably wondering what happens next."

"Yes," said Tobert.

"Joseph, can you borrow the clothes from the bone-pickers and meet us at Naomi's wagon in half an hour?" Pushmataha asked.

"Joseph can't, but I can," said the panther, standing hunched down before us.

Tobert looked back and forth from the panther to us, with the wide eyes of someone seeing the rapid change from human to panther for the first time.

"We'll race you," Pushmataha said.

"You're on," the panther replied, leaping for the tree trunk, sinking his claws into the bark, and disappearing into the pines.

"Are you ready, Tobert?" Pushmataha asked.

Without waiting for him to reply, Pushmataha lifted us all into a swirling cloud of mist. Up and down the trail we sped, through trees and rocky hillsides. Pushmataha wanted Tobert to see firsthand what ghosts can do. We soon settled over the family campsite, floating down and landing softly on the ground.

Everyone but Naomi was asleep.

"Is Nita hoke?" Naomi asked.

"Yes," Pushmataha said. "She is following Pointy Nose and will soon report back to us."

"Where is Joseph?" she asked, looking to the ground in fear.

"He is safe," I said. "He will join us soon."

Without waiting for Naomi to ask what had happened, Pushmataha spoke. "Naomi, wake your parents up," he said. "You need to let them know you are leaving for a few days. We have business to finish in Washington."

I looked to Pushmataha and he returned my glance.

I don't want to see you die, I thought.

Isaac, you and your friends must know what happened to me.

Why?

So it can never happen again, my son.

I will try to be strong, my chief, but I might cry.

So might I, Isaac. So might I.

"Halito," a soft voice called out from the nearby trees.

"I am here," Joseph said. "When are we leaving?"

Naomi awakened her mother and father and whispered words we could not hear. Her mother hugged her tight and fought back her tears. "Please be careful," she said, and Naomi's father gripped her hands and kissed his little girl on the cheek.

"Achukma," Pushmataha announced. "Come close, my Choctaw friends."

"I think I heard my name being called," said Jumper, nipping my heels and wagging his always waggable tail.

"Hoke," said Pushmataha, "you may come as long as you know when to be quiet."

"Not a problem," Jumper said. "I'll just follow the lead of my master, Isaac."

"That's what I'm afraid of."

"Speaking of being afraid, how about some appreciation for what I've done today?" Stella asked, placing her human hands on my ghost shoulders.

"Hoke," said Pushmataha, taking one long breath and looking about the circle. "Anybody else want to come along?"

"Yes, now that you ask," said my big brother, Luke.

Even though we were leaving for a journey into the past—a journey that would end with his death—Chief Pushmataha smiled and welcomed my brother.

"We are quite an army," Pushmataha said, whispering our names. "Naomi, Luke, Joseph, Tobert, Jumper, Isaac, Stella. We will arise and go now."

Chapter 21

A Capitol Offense

AN ARMY OF SEVEN, led by our chief, we sailed over the forest and mountains, watching days and nights come and go—with the speed of blinking fireflies.

As we approached the site of Chief Puckshenubbe's death, we spun into a slow descent. Unable to look away, I saw his body lying among the boulders at the bottom of the cliff. The warm glow of Choctaw ghosts still shone upon the scene, and the horror of his killing called to us like an old, never-to-be-forgotten song.

"Like you," said Pushmataha, "I am saddened by his death. But I did not bring you here to be saddened, or angered."

He stretched out his arms and we joined him, like a family seated around a campfire in the sky. Above us shone a round yellow moon and sparkling stars; below us lay blood-splattered stones.

"Luke," he said. "You are the strong and silent one. Why did I bring you young people here?"

I was so proud of my brother. Without hesitation, he lifted his head and caught us all in his gaze. When he stood to speak, a Luke I never knew existed appeared.

"We are saddened, yes, and angry, too," he said, "but more than that, we are learning. Under your guidance, Pushmataha, we are learning to hold back our anger till the battle is winnable. We are now outnumbered. We have been taken by surprise in the middle of the night. But never again. We will hear the words they do not say and judge more by their actions."

Luke looked at me, shrugged his shoulders, and once again took his seat.

For the longest time, no one said a word. "You have been holding back on us, young man," Pushmataha finally whispered. "If I ever need a speech writer, I think I've found him." In case Luke might see humor in his words, Pushmataha quickly added, "Let us bow our heads. Yakoke. Yakoke for these strong, good Choctaws we are raising."

In what seemed like only a few minutes, we sailed into the morning sun to the east. A wide river flowed below us, and I knew we were almost to Washington.

"To those of you who are still alive," Pushmataha said, "you will notice a difference in the world you are entering. You cannot hide in the trees or disappear in the woods, not here. You will be invisible, just as we are, and nothing is solid to your touch. Do you understand?"

Everyone nodded in response.

"Achukma. Let us now enter Washington, the capital, and the year is 1824."

We slowly floated to the ground, with our feet bouncing up and down. Once everyone was settled, we all took a deep breath and stared in wonder at the big Nahullo city.

"Don't be afraid," Pushmataha said. "No one can see you, and even if they could, they are too busy with their own affairs to notice."

I knew what he meant, but he wasn't exactly speaking the truth. If the people of Washington could see us, they would notice. Five young Choctaws dressed in backwoods clothes, with wide-open mouths and eyes that stared at everything, accompanied by an old woman and a lively talking dog, what was not to notice? They would point at us and laugh and make jokes to themselves, but they would never try to help us.

I remembered my first visit to the cemetery where Pushmataha was buried.

I wonder if we'll go there first? I thought.

No, Isaac. This trip is about my death, but not where I am buried. We are here to learn how and why I died.

If I expected a gun duel or ambush in the night, I was mistaken. Instead, Pushmataha led us to a busy street in the middle of the afternoon. The sidewalks were crowded with hurrying people, and horse-drawn wagons sped by on both sides of the street.

We soon stood before a white stone hotel, with a man in uniform opening and closing the door for well-dressed men and women.

"We could float through the windows like respectable ghosts," he said, "but I want you to experience the city as I saw it."

He followed a young couple through the door, gesturing for us to follow him. We entered the building and stood in awe at the scene before us—colorful paintings, stained-glass windows, shiny wooden floors with bearskin rugs, and a piano standing in the corner.

"You lived here?" I asked.

"Yes, Isaac. I enjoyed all the comforts of the wealthy. Do you see a lesson here?"

Pushmataha looked at Luke and me, then at Naomi.

"Don't be fooled by appearances," she said, and we all nodded.

"Yes," he added. "Do not be blinded by the sparkling lights of wealth."

He led us to a wide stairway, rising and curving to the next floor. We climbed the steps, walked down a long hallway, and paused before a door. The number **27**, carved in dark wood numerals, stared back at us.

With a deep breath and a quick look in our direction, Pushmataha floated through the door and into the room of his death. I had never seen a room so bright and cheerful. Choctaw homes are for gathering in the night and sleeping, and sometimes cooking and eating if the weather is too wet or stormy. But this room had tall glass windows on the wall facing the street. Light blue curtains covered the windows, casting a soft morning color throughout the room.

"Where do you sleep?" I asked.

"Oh, Isaac," he replied. "Did you think this was the only room?"

He ushered us through another door to his bedroom, and before us lay a bed big enough for three Pushmatahas. A wooden nightstand and two puffy chairs filled the room.

"Through that door," Pushmataha said, "is my bathroom. It is where you take your bath and do your private business."

We felt as if we were entering a magic land of wonder, a place beyond the stars—but only for a moment, for we shared a strange and haunting feeling. We were standing in the room of Pushmataha's death.

"What has happened cannot be changed," Pushmataha said. "I ask one thing of you, and I want you to promise me you will do it."

Without waiting for his request, we spoke as one.

"We promise," we said.

"You are promising to see my death, and everything before it, as a great gift—the gift of knowledge. And you must share this gift with all who will listen."

Chapter 22
All that Glitters is Not Gold

WE HEARD PEOPLE making noise in the first room, and when we returned, we were surprised to see the room filled with men and women. The day had become night. Everyone in the room was Nahullo, except for one man who stood taller than the others—Chief Pushmataha. He wore his military uniform from his days as a general in the United States Army.

Joseph, Tobert, and Naomi are still acting like humans, I thought, watching as they moved through the room, pausing to let people pass and wiggling in and out of crowds.

Once Tobert even said, "Excuse me, sir," as he bumped lightly against a man's shoulder.

But not Jumper. He jumped onto the blades of a giant wooden ceiling fan and settled down on all fours. His head rested on his paws, and his nose hung over the side of the fan blade. As the fan spun slowly overhead, his wagging tail greeted us from behind.

"Jumper is home anywhere," I said.

"Way better than me," said Stella. "I don't like being around all these society people. You know what I'd like to do? Turn myself into a rattlesnake and watch them scramble."

"Don't even think about it," Pushmataha said, laughing. We gathered around the living Pushmataha to hear his conversation with three men, each of whom carried an air of importance on his face. They wore coats with tails, and gold watch chains dangled from their pockets.

"Senator Jackson sends his apologies," said the oldest of the men. "He was called to a very important meeting with the president."

"Something about the problem with the Creek Indians in Florida," said a younger man.

"Since when has President Monroe asked for Jackson's advice on anything?" Pushmataha replied, taking a sip from a tall glass.

The three men glanced at each other and looked to the floor. Though Pushmataha didn't notice, I could tell that they were lying.

"No one knows the Creeks better than Senator Andrew Jackson," the oldest man replied.

"If they want to discuss Indians, why didn't they call me?" Pushmataha said. "That's why I was invited to Washington. At least that's what General Jackson said."

"Senator Jackson," said the young man, in a tone meant to correct our chief, "is answering the call of our nation's president. He will see you when he is available."

"I am the leader of a nation as well," Pushmataha said, "the Choctaw Nation, and my people need me. Please tell Jackson his old friend would like to see him."

"Of course I'll tell him," said the eldest of the trio, draping his arm over Pushmataha's shoulder. He smiled and held his glass high. "Now, let's declare a long and happy peace between our nations."

"Hear, hear!" shouted the young man, tapping a spoon to his glass and gaining the attention of everyone. "We are proposing a toast. Raise your glasses high."

The entire room of Nahullos turned their eyes to the older man and waited.

"In honor of General Pushmataha," he said, "who served with Senator Jackson in the war against the British, we wish for a long and happy peace between the Choctaws and the United States of America."

"Hear, hear!" said all, nodding and sipping their golden, sparkling drinks.

Pushmataha joined them, swallowing every drop in his glass. "My glass is empty," he said to a passing servant. The servant glanced nervously at the older Nahullo and rushed to refill Pushmataha's glass.

"What just happened?" I asked.

Ghost Pushmataha looked at me with a sad look. He took a deep breath and spoke to us, his tiny army.

"I want you all to hear this," he said. "Did anyone see

what happened? Do you know what it means?"

"May I speak?" Luke asked.

Pushmataha nodded.

"The men were lying to you. Jackson was not too busy to see you. For some reason, he is making you wait."

"If he didn't want to see you, why did he invite you to Washington?" Naomi asked.

"He said he wanted to talk, like in the old days, and I believed him," said Pushmataha. "But he did not want to talk. He knew I was against our moving, leaving our Choctaw land and homes."

In the silence that followed, we all began to put the events together, everything we had seen—and we dropped our jaws when we recalled the mysterious death of Chief Puckshenubbe.

"I was very close to General Jackson in the war against the British," Pushmataha continued. "We fought to protect New Orleans, along with a thousand Choctaws and the American army. And we won. He knew I was a powerful leader, and that was one reason he did not want to go to war with the Choctaw Nation."

As we stood in Pushmataha's hotel room, twenty people, maybe more, laughed and talked and enjoyed the evening. Servants moved about the room, carrying trays of sandwiches and what looked like cookies.

"How many of them know they are here to deceive you, to walk you to your grave?" I whispered.

"I don't care how many of them know," Pushmataha said. "The only one I care about is absent."

With these words the room grew dark. No city lights shone through the window; no sparkling stars danced in the sky. We soon floated into another room, a smaller room in another building. Three men sat around a table, pouring drinks from a large jug.

"He's a tough one, too hardheaded to reason with," said a white-haired man who sat with his legs crossed.

"That's him, isn't it," I asked Pushmataha, "and he's talking about you?"

"Yes, Isaac, that is the man I knew as General Jackson, my closest friend."

Chapter 23
Dark Night Deathwalk

WE KNEW THIS WAS a time to listen. We looked upon a man, Senator Andrew Jackson from the state of Tennessee, who would someday be president of the United States of America. I shivered and wrapped my arms around myself. I was hungry to know what this man Jackson said to his closest friends—when no one else could hear.

As I recalled my Choctaw friends, those who had died in the fires and by the smallpox and on the Trail, I was hit with one thought. The man sitting before us brought about their deaths—and my death, too.

The truth is not always easy to swallow, and you are here to learn the truth, Pushmataha replied.

We nodded and huddled closer to the four men.

"He is so stubborn," Jackson said, shaking his head.

"And he says he will never allow the Choctaws to leave their land in Mississippi."

"Aren't there other Choctaws who would listen to us?" asked a younger man sitting across the table from Jackson.

"Yes, but not as long as Pushmataha is alive, for he's not alone. He led a battalion of a thousand Choctaw soldiers during the war," Jackson said. "When they left the army, after the war was over, I let them keep their weapons."

"So the Choctaws are armed?" a man in a black suit asked.

"Well-armed," said Jackson. "And the man who still rules their every action is Pushmataha."

"Have you tried to talk to him lately?" Black Suit asked.

"As if that would do any good!" said the Younger.

"It's worth a try," replied Black Suit.

"Maybe," said Jackson. "Maybe."

He cast his eyes slowly from one man to the other, until they knew the importance of what he was about to say. We invisible listeners, Pushmataha and his army, knew that Jackson's next words carried a quiet and venomous blade, a knife to the heart of who we are as Choctaws.

"Once Pushmataha is gone," he said, "they will be helpless. We'll destroy their towns, their homes, and they won't know what to do. The land will be ours."

"And you have a plan to get rid of Pushmataha?"

"Oh, no," said Jackson. "I would never do anything so heinous as to harm a fellow soldier. But he has certain weaknesses about the food he eats. I have spoken to the chef about his diet. Pushmataha has, it seems, various allergies."

"Allergies to what?" asked the Younger.

"Seafood, among others," said Jackson. "After a dinner of shrimp one night in New Orleans, I watched him almost die. His face turned red and he passed out and fell to the floor."

"A brilliant plan," said Black Suit. "No guns, no blood, a natural death."

"A diet of seafood, a little at a time," said Jackson. "He'll never make it out of Washington alive."

Jackson lifted his glass high, as if toasting his intentions. The others joined him, nodding and laughing as they sipped the golden brew.

"How can you watch this?" Tobert asked.

"It is painful, I admit, but this is not for me alone. I have seen this already," said Pushmataha. "I want you, all of you, to know the man who gives the orders, the man who burned your homes."

"The man who gave my grandparents the blankets," Joseph said.

"The man behind my capture," said Naomi.

"The true leader," said Luke.

"This man deserves my venom," Stella said.

"He has the venom of his own life," said Pushmataha. "We all must live with what we do, and his life is a very unhappy one."

The room turned dark once more, and we rose above the hotel, above the city of Washington, and far below we watched the blinking, blazing lights of nightfall in the city. I felt myself floating down, landing with my friends on the soft carpet of the hotel lobby.

"I waited for almost a month for him to see me," said Pushmataha. "I almost stopped eating. One night, after two weeks in Washington, I woke up at three o'clock in the morning. I was more wide awake than ever. I rolled out of bed and climbed downstairs to the hotel lobby."

We joined Pushmataha at the bottom of the stairs, watching the living chief approach the front desk of the hotel.

"Has anyone left me any messages?"

The desk clerk looked up in surprise.

"No, General, not at this hour."

"Yakoke," Pushmataha said, then corrected himself. "Oh, I'm sorry. I meant to say thank you."

"You are welcome, sir," said the clerk. "Is there anything I can do for you?"

"No, I think I'll go for a walk. There is a park nearby, with woods and a small lake, am I right?"

"Yes, two blocks to your left after you leave the hotel. But sir, it is well after midnight. The streets are not safe at this hour. You should not be out alone."

"Thank you for the warning," Pushmataha said. "But I'll be hoke." He pulled back his coat and tapped a hatchet, a Choctaw stone hatchet, tucked inside his belt.

The attendant nodded. "Ahhh," he said. "I hope you know what you are doing."

The doorman slept in a chair near the entrance, not expecting anyone to be about at such an hour. Pushmataha pushed open the heavy door and stepped to the sidewalk. Once outside, he lifted his arms to the sky and took a deep breath. The stars twinkled in response and a thin sliver of moon peeked from the clouds to say halito. Pushmataha looked up and down the sidewalk and, seeing no one, turned in the direction of the woods.

"Wait," said Ghost Pushmataha. "Look to the lobby." Through the glass window we spotted two very familiar men, the sergeant and corporal from the wagon that had carried Chief Puckshenubbe to his death.

"Those are the men who killed Chief Puckshenubbe," I whispered. "What are they doing here?"

"They are keeping an eye on you, aren't they?" asked Luke.

"Yes, they are following me and reporting everything I do to Jackson."

"Did you know they were watching you?" Tobert asked.

Pushmataha said nothing. As we watched, the men hurried to the front desk to speak to the clerk.

"Where is he going?" asked the sergeant.

"He asked for directions to the park," the clerk replied. "I told him it was dangerous after dark, but he didn't seem worried. He showed me his hatchet, so be careful."

The sergeant laughed. "I think two men with guns are a match for an old Indian with a hatchet," he said

They exited the hotel and followed Pushmataha, staying hidden in the shadows. Pushmataha took the pathway into the park, a dark and heavily wooded stretch of land beside the river.

"Where were you going?" I asked Pushmataha.

"To the capitol," he said. "This was the year, 1824,

when the new United States capitol was still being built. I wanted to see it."

"In the middle of the night?" Naomi asked. "Why?"

"I had a mission. I was not carrying the hatchet for my protection."

We knew Pushmataha would tell us his purpose when he was ready, so we remained silent and watched. The living Pushmataha took a long and winding path deep into the woods, till the new capitol appeared in the distance, across a bridge. As he stood beneath the shadow of an old oak tree, the sergeant and corporal snuck up behind him.

"He is serving himself on a silver platter," the sergeant whispered.

"What do you mean?' asked the corporal.

"We can kill him now. Not with guns, they'll make too much noise. But with this," the sergeant said, pulling a long-bladed knife from his scabbard. The moonlight shone on the sharp blade as he held it high.

"We were told to keep him alive, till he dies of natural causes."

"But now's our chance," said the sergeant. "He spoke to the desk clerk, who will testify he warned him not to go outside this late."

"What do we do with his body?" asked the corporal.

"That's the easy part," said the sergeant. "We take whatever he has of value—a watch, jewelry, money—and people will think he was killed by thieves. We leave his body here and someone will find him in the morning."

"I don't like it," said the corporal. "We had orders."

"So you would rather follow orders and stay in that hotel and wait for him to die? We can take care of the problem now. I'll do it. You just keep your gun handy and stay quiet."

I looked around me, at the circle of Choctaw friends surrounding ghost Pushmataha. Joseph was now the panther. Stella was her rattlesnake self, wrapped in a circle and flicking her poisonous fangs at the night air.

"I am still ashamed of many things I did in my life," Pushmataha said. "But watch closely." His lips rose in a slight smile.

"What is about to happen?" I asked. "Is this how you die? Please, I do not want to see this."

"Yes you do, Isaac," he replied. "Yes, you do."

The sergeant took a deep breath and raised his knife shoulder high. With each careful step, he moved closer to his intended target, the neck of Pushmataha. Making no sound, nothing to warn our chief, the sergeant nodded his head like a bull about to charge. As both hands gripped the knife handle, he stood on tiptoe and readied himself to plunge the blade into our beloved chief and end his life.

Pushmataha coughed and stumbled two steps forward, and for just a moment the sergeant paused.

Chapter 24

From Nanih Waiya to the Capitol

THAT MOMENT was enough. Pushmataha spun around and faced his attacker. With his left arm, he knocked the knife from the sergeant's hand. Pushmataha gripped a pistol and held it against the chest of Sergeant Hill.

"Where is the corporal?" Pushmataha asked.

"I am here alone," the sergeant lied.

"You tried to kill me, and unless you want to die, tell your friend to come out where I can see him. And tell him to drop his gun." The look on Pushmataha's face was one the soldiers had never seen before. "You think I didn't know you were watching me?" he said. "Now, call the corporal."

"Here I am," the corporal said, stepping from the shadows. Pushmataha pulled the sergeant in front of him, as a shield.

"Throw your gun to the ground," Pushmataha said. The corporal tossed his pistol to the forest floor. "Now take the sergeant's gun, too, and throw it to the ground."

The corporal did as he was told.

"You don't understand what's happening," the sergeant said.

"I know exactly what is happening," Pushmataha said. "General Jackson sent you, didn't he?"

"Yes," said the sergeant. "He sent us to watch out for you."

"Then why were you hiding?"

"Senator Jackson, or General Jackson, as you know him, did not want to insult you," the sergeant said. "He knew you would say you have no need for guards, that you can take care of yourself. But he wants to make sure you are safe."

"So you were protecting me with a knife at my back?" Pushmataha said, stooping to pick up the knife. "And you are watching me every hour of the day?"

"Yes. Jackson knows you like to walk alone. At night."

"If you are telling me the truth," said Pushmataha, "then prove it. Turn around and head back to the hotel. I will keep your weapons for now. I will see you in a hour in the lobby, and you can get your guns back then."

"Senator Jackson will be very angry with us. We can't do that."

"Oh yes you can! Turn yourselves around and go! And if you try to sneak up on me again tonight, I still have your guns. And I will give them to General Jackson tomorrow."

"We'd better do what he says," the corporal said. "We don't have a choice."

The sergeant nodded and then—with a mean glare at Pushmataha—he took the corporal by the arm and turned him around, facing the path to the hotel.

"I will keep my gun at your back," Pushmataha said to the sergeant. "And if the corporal tries to run, I'll let him go."

"And you will shoot me," said the sergeant.

"You are a smart man," Pushmataha said. "I am still a soldier, and I am here representing the Choctaw Nation. With your actions tonight, you are our enemy."

With those words, Pushmataha nudged his pistol in the sergeant's back and led his two attackers through the woods to the sidewalk. We all followed, surrounding our Pushmataha with pride.

Stella spoke first to begin our celebration.

Whrrrr. Whrrrr.

Panther Joseph leapt to a thick tree limb and swatted at the sergeant as he walked past. His claws flew through the air, of course, without touching anything, but we cheered anyway.

Luke patted Pushmataha on the back. "We had no idea you knew they were following you. I bet you were a great general."

"That's what everyone says," added Naomi.

"And everyone is right," I whispered.

"At least for tonight," Pushmataha said, nodding his head in humility. "But the evening is not over yet."

163

Pushmataha stood on the sidewalk and waited as the sergeant and corporal entered the hotel. He peered through the window as they climbed the stairs, then turned quickly and hurried down the path once more.

He neared the foundation of the new capitol, the granite structure that would replace the old wooden capitol, the building burned by the British during the War of 1812.

As we watched, I glanced at Ghost Pushmataha. The memories were flying through his mind, I knew.

"That is why I decided to join the American army," he said, speaking softly in my ear.

"Why?"

He pointed once more to the capitol, but what we saw was not the heavy stone foundation of today's capitol. No, we—all of us, Stella, Joseph, Naomi, Luke, Tobert, Jumper, Pushmataha, and I—stared at the burning capitol of the war, the flames rising from the burning capitol, the first capitol of the new nation, the United States of America.

British soldiers surrounded the wooden structure as the wind whipped the fire and orange and red embers flew with the crash and fall of every board. The British soldiers stood at attention, as if they guarded a coronation of a new king and queen. They stood in pride and watched the capitol building, the house of independence, fall to the ground.

"I did not want to see this again. I have watched it far too many times," said Pushmataha. "But you must see what they did. You must know."

We all felt the anger of Pushmataha, and for the

first time understood his determination to fight alongside General Jackson at the Battle of New Orleans. This
night belonged to our general, and with a skyward wave
of his right arm time flew by, a year at least for every
second.

We watched as the fire died, the British disappeared,
the trees returned, the stars and moon and sun blinked
and blinded us, till we remembered to cover our eyes. But
we wanted so much to see!

As time slowed, American soldiers dug deep holes
where the capitol now stood, digging the bottom floors of
the building we know today. They carried dirt in wagons
and piled it in mountains of soil nearby, ready to use as the
new building was constructed.

With another wave of Pushmataha's arm, we returned to
the night of his journey. Leaving the hotel and the soldiers
behind, Pushmataha cut a new path, through the woods
surrounding the capitol.

As he neared the thick foundation, waiting for the
building that would someday sit atop it, he reached into his
pocket and removed the stone hatchet.

He circled the foundation in a slow and thoughtful
walk, tapping the hatchet in the palm of his hand.

"Do you know where I found the hatchet?" Ghost
Pushmataha asked.

No one spoke, till once again the *whirring* of Stella's
rattlesnake tail whispered in reply. "Nanih Waiya," she
said, and the air vibrated with the sound of our sacred
Choctaw mound, a hundred-foot-tall mound of deep,

dark earth—filled with the bones of our Choctaw ancestors.

"Yes," he nodded. "After the Battle of New Orleans, I returned home to Choctaw Nation, Mississippi. I was grateful to be alive, and one Saturday afternoon I rode my horse to the banks of the river Bok Chitto, across the road from Nanih Waiya. I built a small fire and slept on the riverbank with my blanket curled tight around me. My United States Army blanket.

"The next morning, I woke up before sunrise and crossed the road. The ground was muddy from a heavy rainfall a few days before. As I climbed the mound, I slipped and fell and rolled down the slope. My boot struck something as I skidded to a stop."

"It was the hatchet?" I asked.

"Yes, Isaac, it was the hatchet. An ancient stone hatchet, no doubt carried with the bones of our ancestors and buried in the mound we call Nanih Waiya."

"And you brought it here, to the American capital?"

"And why would I do that?" Pushmataha asked.

"As a show of peace between our nations," Naomi said.

"I am so proud to be here with you young people," Pushmataha whispered, and we could all feel the tears filling his eyes and rolling gently down his cheeks. "I am so comforted, knowing you will lead our people."

Well, some of us will lead, I thought, *but some of us have no lives to lead with anymore.*

"You have been more of a leader, my son, since you

left your body behind," Pushmataha answered, once again reading my mind.

Chapter 25

But Not Forever Death

WE WATCHED ONCE more as Pushmataha circled the foundation of the new capitol, till he came to a spot facing east. A pathway, at least a hundred feet wide, stretched well into the surrounding woods.

"This will be a stairway leading to the main entrance," Ghost Pushmataha whispered. "It will be a safe place for the hatchet, as the ground is ready for the rock foundation. And all who walk these steps will be blessed by the Choctaw hatchet."

Stella—sweet and funny Rattlesnake Stella—went first, diving to the ground and wriggling in the dirt.

We all followed, digging up the hard dirt with our fingers. Joseph dug with his panther claws and Jumper with his puppy-dog paws.

We didn't move a single speck of dirt, of course, for we are from the future.

With a soft *whirr*, Stella retreated, and so did we all. We huddled together as Pushmataha knelt and paused, as if in prayer. With the palms of his hands he dug a hole in the rough dirt, two feet deep at least. He clutched the hatchet, his left hand on the stone head and his right hand on the handle, and raised it high, lifting it to the heavens. Then he lowered it to the grave.

Yes, that is what we saw.

Not a hole in the dirt, but a gravesite, a burial of this sacred hatchet into a living grave of peace. Still kneeling, he cupped dirt in his hands and scattered it over the gravesite till it was covered. He then raked and smoothed the ground, rocking back and forth with every gesture.

Ghost Pushmataha turned to us, saying, "Now you know the depth of my feelings, which I hope you will someday share. But we are not finished here."

With a slow-at-first rising and falling of the sun, the moon and sun danced in the sky, and we took a ghostly breath and readied ourselves for a dizzying dash through time. But only a few days passed, and we settled inside Pushmataha's hotel room.

"I finally did see General Jackson," he said. "On the last day of my life. I was too sick to crawl out of bed, so he came to me."

In a flash, we stood in the hallway, where Andrew Jackson waited for a hotel employee to open the door to Pushmataha's room. He was surrounded by several important-looking men in suits. "Senators," said Jackson, "do not be alarmed by the sight of Chief Pushmataha. He is very ill, and I fear on his deathbed. He has asked for us to hear his final wishes."

The senators nodded and bowed their heads, then followed Jackson into the room. Jackson knocked on the door to the bedroom and a familiar voice answered.

"Yes, who is it?" asked the sergeant.

"It is I, Senator Jackson, along with others from the government." Sergeant Hill hurried to the door, opened it quickly, and cast his eyes to Jackson, waiting for his orders.

"Gather chairs around the bed and step outside," said Jackson.

The sergeant did as he was told and exited the room, shutting the door behind him. The senators watched as Jackson took the chair closest to Pushmataha.

"Halito," said Jackson, leaning over the bed where Pushmataha lay, his eyes closed.

We felt a shiver, a cold and helpless shiver, as our most respected chief lifted his head from the pillow. His face was bright red and swollen, and he could barely open his eyes.

"What is happening?" he whispered. "You are here? In my room?"

"Yes, my friend, I have come to see you."

Pushmataha dug his elbows into the bed and pushed himself to a seated position. "I am sorry I'm not dressed," he said. "Give me a few minutes."

"No, no," said Jackson. "You need to stay in bed. You are not well. I have brought my fellow senators to meet you."

Pushmataha shook his head slowly back and forth. "No, I am not well," he said. "I am afraid I will never rise from this bed alive, General Jackson. The doctors say they can do nothing to help me. Thank you so much for coming to see me."

Jackson reached for Pushmataha's hand and held it tight. "Is there anything you would like to say?" he asked.

Pushmataha nodded and coughed. We all waited, knowing these might be the final words ever spoken by the living Chief Pushmataha, our friend and powerful leader. When Pushmataha raised his head and opened his eyes, he did not look like a man about to die. The Pushmataha we knew, the strong chief who know no fears—this was the man who now lay before us.

He took a deep breath and locked eyes with everyone in the room before speaking. "I will be brief," he said, "but harken to my words."

The senators stepped closer, knowing they would never forget this moment.

"I can say, and speak the truth, that neither I nor my father nor any of my ancestors ever drew bow in anger against the people of the United States. We have been true in our friendship; we have held your hands so long that our fingers, like the claws of an eagle, will not let them go. And we shall never draw arms against you."

After a long pause, Jackson leaned close to Pushmataha and whispered, "What is your last request?"

"Bury me with the big guns firing over the grave," said Pushmataha.

Jackson bowed his head, as did the other senators, but they never saw what we witnessed.

We were soon joined by the ghosts of so many Choctaws from the past, many from our deadly walk, and they were young and old and my age, too. Even Chief Puckshenubbe appeared. We filled the room, from floor to ceiling, welcoming Chief Pushmataha to our home, the Land of Ghosts.

Suddenly, in this holy gathering, I had an unholy thought. It would not go away. Maybe it was the way Jackson had said "halito" when he greeted Pushmataha, as if he were his closest friend.

The answer to Pushmataha's death and burial in the cemetery at Washington now opened before me, as clear as the sunrise over the mountains.

"May I speak?" I asked.

Pushmataha, I knew, had already read my mind.

"Yes, Isaac, you may offer a new way of seeing my death."

"If the plantation owners of the South, Jackson's people, were to have the land they wanted to grow more cotton, the Choctaws had to move," I said. "And if you, Chief Pushmataha, were so against this move, you must be gone, out of the way."

Pushmataha slowly turned his head in my direction. His eyes were full of tears.

"That is why you never returned from Washington?" I asked.

"Yes, Isaac, I fear you speak the truth," said Pushmataha.

"And what about the hatchet, the hatchet of peace between our nations?"

Everyone gathered close. We felt the strength of thousands of Choctaw ghosts, surrounding us as part of the circle. Chief Puckshenubbe, who died before he reached Washington, and ghosts from the fires that burned our homes joined the thin-faced Choctaw ghosts who died of starvation on the trail.

But these were not ghosts—no! They were not the kind of ghosts most people think about, something to be afraid of, something to run away from. They were and are people—Choctaw people, mothers and fathers and sons and daughters. They are us.

Naomi spoke the words we felt.

"We should leave the Choctaw hatchet," Naomi said. "Leave it buried in the foundation of this new nation, for the goodness of a people cannot be undone by the deeds of one. We want peace between our nations, and we must leave the hatchet buried."

"And so we shall," said Pushmataha.

Chapter 26

Jones Academy Indian Boarding School
Choctaw Nation, 2018

"MRS. CHARLES?"

"Yes, Robbie?"

"This is too weird."

"What is too weird?"

"This book I'm reading. It's weird."

"What are you reading?"

"*When A Ghost Talks, Listen.*"

"Why is it weird? People are time-traveling, there are ghosts and shape-shifters. That's not unusual in fiction for your age group."

"I'm not talking about that. I'm talking about reading a book about reading a book in Jones Academy, and here I am reading the book in Jones Academy. And ghosts from the book are supposed to be floating around the library, where we are, right now, watching me read about them.

You have to admit—that is weird!" Robbie exclaimed.

"If you don't want to read it, let me have it," Sherry said.

"No way!"

"Robbie," said Mrs. Charles, "if you're reading about Jones Academy, you're almost finished. Sherry, you can have the book tomorrow."

"Yakoke," said Sherry, smiling at Robbie.

"Hoke, help me out here," Robbie said. "Is all of this stuff true? Did Andrew Jackson invite Chief Pushmataha to Washington, D.C., to kill him? Why would a senator do that?"

Mrs. Charles slowly stood before replying. She lifted her arms high and spoke in a voice loud enough for every student in the library to hear. "Put down your books," she said. "I want everyone to listen to what I am about to say. First, let me say that I respect you, all of you, more than you could ever know. You are good readers and you are thoughtful readers. You want to know the truth.

"You have heard me say over and over how important it is to think about what you read. Do not accept anything as absolutely true, whether the book is fiction or nonfiction. You must think first, and then you must research. Research online, research in libraries, research in archives.

"And if the subject is of high interest to you, such as the Trail of Tears or the history of Indian boarding schools, never stop researching. Always, somewhere lies an unturned stone, a hidden truth." Robbie raised his hand again and Mrs. Charles motioned for him to lower it.

"I want to say something about the How I Became A Ghost books, especially Book Two, *When A Ghost Talks, Listen*. These books are fiction, which means many events are made up. The shape-shifting Rattlesnake Stella, Joseph the Panther Boy, and time-traveling, these are far from what we accept as truth today. But the violence and cruelty on the Trail of Tears, as you and your families know, are often underplayed.

"The court cases and treaty signings and corruption by government officials during Indian Removal—all of that is well-documented. How deep did the corruption go? Did it involve murder, as the book suggests? Maybe you will never know for certain.

"I will not attempt to answer your questions about the death of Pushmataha. That I will leave up to you. Research and ask—question teachers, writers, professors, dive into the history and come to your own conclusion."

"Please, Mrs. Charles," said Robbie, without raising his hand, "can't you give us some little hint about where to go, what books to read? Remember, we're Indians, what do we know about libraries and books?"

Every student laughed and nodded and called out one stereotype after another.

"I live in a teepeeee," said one.

"Yeah, and I chase buffalo!" said another.

"And I got a new can of war paint for my birthday," said a power forward on the girls basketball team.

Mrs. Charles place her hands on her hips and gave Robbie her most threatening look-what-you-started stare.

"I'm sorry," Robbie replied, "but give us some little idea, at least. I'll do the research, just help me get started."

Mrs. Charles took a deep breath and cast her eyes around the room. Thirty-seven students of Jones Academy waited for her response. She was so proud of them she wanted to cry.

Finally she spoke. "An obscure little pamphlet of a book is a good starting place," she said. "It is written by one of my college professors, Dr. David Baird, and the title is *The Choctaw People*. And be sure to read page thirty-two."

"Wow!" said Robbie. "You remember the page number?"

Mrs. Charles bowed her head as students hurried to the computers, looking for the location of the book.

"Robbie, you will never forget the page number either, once you read what it says," she whispered.

"Why did the author set the final chapter of this book in Jones Academy?" Robbie asked.

"How many of you have read this book? *When A Ghost Talks, Listen?*" Mrs. Charles asked, and at least a dozen students raised their hands.

"Excellent. I think Mr. Tingle wrote about Jones Academy because he respects you. He knows your lives have not been easy, and he is proud of how hard you are working. Maybe he sees a little of Isaac in Jones Academy students."

"And Naomi," said one student.

"And Nita," said another.

"And Joseph," said a football player.

"He could have dedicated the book to Jones Academy students," Robbie said. "That would be cool."

"If you turn to the front of the book, you'll see that he did," said Mrs. Charles.

"Hey, we have a book dedicated to us!" said a student. "I want to read it."

"Me, too," said at least a dozen more students, waving their hands as they dashed across the room to read the dedication.

"All right already!" shouted Mrs. Charles. "Settle down, please. Robbie, bring me the book. Boys and girls, if you can behave for . . . oh, let's say five minutes, think you can do that?"

Thirty-seven heads bobbed up and down in silent agreement. "Good," she said. "Let's move to the theater room, and I will read the first chapter to everyone."

The theater room was adjacent to the library, and three rows of bleacher-style seats circled the room and faced a wall where the speaker sat or stood. Author visits, though seldom, were usually held in this room.

Mrs. Charles smiled as she opened the door. She loved sharing passages from her favorite books, in hopes that her listeners would be inspired to read the books for themselves. The students gathered behind her, ready to enter the room. But as so often happens in life, the unexpected ruled the day.

Mrs. Charles froze. Her eyes widened and her jaw dropped. She took four quick breaths and took a step backwards. Thirty-seven students crowded around her, leaping and kneeling and poking their heads around the door to see what she saw.

Chapter 27
Icy Trail and Back Again

NO ONE SAID A WORD, till finally Robbie lifted his right hand over Mrs. Charles's shoulder and counted from one to eight—in Choctaw and ever so slowly. "Achufa, tuklo, tukchina, ushta, tahlapi, hannali, untuklo, untuchina."

No one asked what he was counting.

Everyone saw us, eight Choctaws from the past floating before their very eyes.

"Chief Pushmataha," whispered Sherry, "just like the picture on Mr. Randell's wall."

Chief Pushmataha smiled and nodded, and the students gasped. "Wow . . ."

As if the appearance of eight characters from the book was not strange enough, Stella curled up on the floor a few feet away—as a rattlesnake.

"Stella?" Robbie asked.

Whrrrrrr came the soft reply.

"You too, Joseph?" he said, staring at the teenager in front of him.

Joseph bowed his head and lifted his hands in front of his chest, opening and closing his fists till his fingers became claws. Fur sprouted from his face and arms, his legs grew lean, and he finally settled on the floor. The eyes of a black panther gazed at the students of Jones Academy.

Ruff! Ruff!—came the sound, and all eyes turned to Jumper, wagging his tail in a corner of the room.

Mrs. Charles took another deep breath and regained her strength.

"We are so honored to welcome you to Jones Academy," she said.

"Halito," Robbie said, and soon *halito* was repeated so many times, over and over, that Chief Pushmataha smiled and nudged me.

"I think I'm supposed to say something," I said, "but I am as surprised as you are. What year is it?"

"It's today! It's now," said Robbie. "Oh, sorry. Uh, it is 2018. The year is 2018."

"We've come a long way," said Luke. "We just left 1824."

"Step inside the room," Chief Pushmataha said. "And Mrs. Charles, may we close the door?"

"Of course."

The students stepped through the door and settled on

the bleachers. As soon as the last student entered the room, the door closed slowly by itself. Jumper the dog, Rattlesnake Stella, and Panther Joseph joined Luke, Naomi, Tobert, and me. We surrounded Chief Pushmataha as everyone waited for the next surprise.

"You are about to see things you have never seen before," he said, "but I will guarantee your safety. No need to be afraid."

Mrs. Charles looked from left to right, telling her students to be strong—telling them with her eyes. The room went suddenly dark and the smell of smoke was strong. Flames danced overhead and burning boards fell from the ceiling.

Students screamed and huddled together, and in a flash, the fires were gone, the sun rose, a cloudy blue sky shone above them, and snow began to fall. For what seemed like days, the Jones Academy students and their librarian joined the Choctaw eight on the Trail of Tears, freezing and struggling to stay alive.

"I have never been so cold in my life," Robbie said, shivering as he spoke.

As darkness came and brought howling winds and sheets of rain, moans filled the room, and students cried out loud, unashamed.

"My family went through this."

"No wonder so many people died."

"I want this to be over."

Chief Pushmataha hovered over the room, and with a slow wave of his arms the icy trail finally vanished. Once more the sun shone through the windows of the Jones Academy library.

"Is everyone hoke?" Mrs. Charles asked.

She shook her head, and a thin icicle dropped to the carpet. Before anyone could answer, the sound of a thousand voices filled every corner of the room, Choctaw voices singing our Choctaw song.

"Shilombish holitopama," they sang, and many students joined them. They sang as American soldiers carried a coffin down the streets of the nation's capital. Through the shiny coffin boards everyone saw the body of Chief Pushmataha.

"No time for sadness," said the chief. "I will be with you always. And now for the next chapter of our journey, the next book waiting to be written."

From a distance came the loud popping of gunfire, and the room shivered with the dark winds of night on a foreign shore. Soldiers climbed from muddy trenches and attacked enemy troops.

A thin beam of moonlight shone on a single soldier, huddled against the stone wall of a graveyard.

"His name is Joseph Oklahombi," Chief Pushmataha said. "And you will know him well. My friends and I will leave you now. If you need us, we will always be here for you—within the pages of your favorite book."

Eight Choctaws, some of us living and some of us ghosts, floated over the students of Jones Academy, waving slowly and whispering "chipisha latchiki, we will see you again," as we disappeared.

"Pushmataha?" I asked.

"Yes, Isaac?"

"I have to agree with Robbie."

"What do you mean?"

"This is weird."

Research Bibliography

Baird, W. David. *The Choctaw People*. Phoenix: Indian Tribal Series, 1973.

Jahoda, Gloria. *The Trail of Tears: The Story of the America Indian Removals 1813-1855*. Wings Books, a division of Random House, 1975.

Lincecum, Gideon. *Pushmataha: A Choctaw Leader and his People*. University of Alabama Press, 2004.

Remini, Robert V. *Andrew Jackson and his Indian Wars*. Penguin Books, 2001.

About the Author

Tim Tingle is an Oklahoma Choctaw storyteller and an award-winning author of nineteen books. His great-great-grandfather, John Carnes, walked the Trail of Tears in 1835, and his grandmother attended rigorous Indian boarding schools in the early 1900s. In 1992, he retraced the Trail of Tears to Mississippi and began recording stories of tribal elders. His family experiences and these interviews with fellow Choctaws in Texas, Alabama, Mississippi, and Oklahoma—more than two hundred hours and counting—are the basis of his most important writings.

His first children's book, *Crossing Bok Chitto*, was an Oklahoma Sequoyah Award Finalist and an Editor's Choice in the New York Times Book Review. Tingle was a featured author and speaker at the 2014 National Book Festival in Washington, D.C., based on the critical acclaim for *How I Became a Ghost*, which won the 2014 American Indian Library Association Youth Literature Award.

Tingle received his master's degree in English Literature at the University of Oklahoma in 2003, with a focus on American Indian studies. While teaching freshmen writing courses and completing his thesis, "Choctaw Oral Literature," Tingle wrote his first book, *Walking the Choctaw Road*. It was selected by both Oklahoma and Alaska as their Book of the Year for the "One Book, One State" program. As a visiting author, Tingle reaches audiences numbering more than 200,000 annually, and in April of 2018 was awarded the Arrell Gibson Lifetime Achievement Award by the Oklahoma Center for the Book, a state affiliate of the Center for the Book in the Library of Congress.